ISBN 978-1-331-46954-4
PIBN 10194440

1 MONTH OF
FREE
READING

at

www.ForgottenBooks.com

By purchasing this book you are eligible for one month membership to ForgottenBooks.com, giving you unlimited access to our entire collection of over 700,000 titles via our web site and mobile apps.

To claim your free month visit:

www.forgottenbooks.com/free194440

Similar Books Are Available from
www.forgottenbooks.com

BURNS IN ENGLISH.

SELECT POEMS

OF

ROBERT BURNS.

Translated from the Scottish Dialect

BY

ALEXANDER CORBETT.

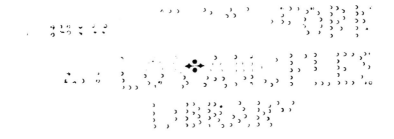

BOSTON:

ALEXANDER CORBETT.

1892.

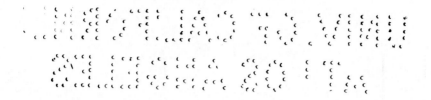

INDEX.

SONGS.

INTRODUCTION.

That the dialect poems of Burns are not easily understood by English readers has been conceded by many eminent writers. Allan Cunningham remarks, " The greater part of his earlier poems are written in the dialect of his country, which is obscure, if not unintelligible, to Englishmen." Cowper writes, " Poor Burns loses much of his deserved praise in this country (England) through our ignorance of his language. I despair of meeting with any Englishman who will take the pains that I have taken to understand him. His candle is bright, but shut up in a dark lantern."

In an edition of " Select Poems of Burns," recently published by Andrew Lang, he says, " To English students, Robert Burns is, and must be, a foreign classic. People who decline to read the Waverley novels because they " detest dialect," must find the author of " Tam o' Shanter " impossible. With the best will in the world, it is tedious to look up glossaries a dozen times on each page, or to desert the text for the foot-notes twice or thrice in a line." Again he says, " His Scotch poems are, by universal consent as well as in his own opinion, infinitely his best poems." We cannot expect

English-speaking nations to make the Scottish dia-
lect a study. Is it not better, then, to help Mahomet
on his way to the mountain, than to expect the
mountain will ever come to Mahomet?

This translation (I use the word for lack of
better) is not, from its limited character, designed
to compete with or supersede Burns' complete
works. The songs are by far the noblest of his
productions. His letters, also, are very interesting
reading. Then again, the essays and biographies
by so many eminent writers, that accompany the
best editions of his works, will always make these
editions sought after.

It is well nigh impossible to translate the songs,
even if it were desirable; I have, therefore, only
attempted to change a few of them.

The most familiar of the poems are written in a
measure that requires four words to rhyme in a
verse of six lines. To have tried to merely substi-
tute an English word for a Scotch one would have
been abortive. I have, therefore, used a free lance,
and changed the rhyme, and occasionally the sense,
to suit the exigency. I have also taken the liberty
to modernize and alter the meaning of allusions in
a few cases. The rhyme will often be found imper-
fect, but the " Bard's " delinquency in that respect is
perhaps a trifle worse than my own. " The life is more
than meat, and the body is more than raiment."

Much of his life and character can be gathered
from his poems. I will only allude briefly to the
main facts of his career. He was born on the 25th
of January, 1759, and died in July, 1796. A hum-

ble cottage was the scene of his birth, about two miles from the town of Ayr, in Scotland. His life from boyhood was one of toil and often privation. About his twenty-seventh year, a series of untoward circumstances made him resolve to leave for Jamaica. He was on his way to the embarking place, when he received a letter from Dr. Blacklock of Edinburgh inviting him to that city. He went there shortly after, and was well received by men and women of note.

﹖A second edition of his poems was published, which brought him about five hundred pounds. He settled on a farm subsequently, and was married to Miss Armour — the " Bonnie Jean " of his song. Later, he got a situation of minor duties and emoluments in the excise, retired from the farm, and made his home in the town of Dumfries, where his final sickness and death took place, and where a splendid mausoleum marks his resting place.

Carlyle, in a review of his life, says, " No poet of any age or nation is more graphic than Burns ; three lines from his hand and we have a likeness,— and in that rough dialect, in that rude, often awkward metre, so clear and definite a likeness ! "

I will make no remarks on his character ; it is a trite subject at best ; but will quote two stanzas of a poem by David Macbeth Moir, who was present at the great Burns' Festival in Ayr, in 1844.

> " Judge not ye, whose thoughts are fingers
>   Of the hands that witch the lyre —
> Greenland has its mountain icebergs,
>   Ætna has its heart of fire ;

Calculation has its plummet,
  Self-control its iron rules;
Genius has its sparkling fountains,
  Dulness has its stagnant pools:
Like a halcyon on the waters,
  Burns' chart disdained a plan;
In his soarings he was heavenly,
  In his sinkings he was man.

As the sun from out the orient
  Pours a wider, warmer light,
Till he floods both earth and ocean,
  Blazing from the zenith's height;
So the glory of our Poet,
  In his deathless power serene,
Shines, as rolling time advances,
  Warmer felt, and wider seen:
First Doon's banks and braes contained it,
  Then his country formed its span;
Now the wide world is its empire,
  And its throne the heart of man."

In conclusion, I hope that the lines of the peasant bard, in these his best effusions, will give a degree of pleasure to those who are not " To the manor born "; and I trust that my Scotch friends will find the general tenor of the poems less changed than might have been expected at first thought.

One thing I have experienced in reading Burns' poems is, that they never grow stale; the " spark of Nature's fire " that runs through the lines is always original, always refreshing.

A. Corbett

BURNS IN ENGLISH.

THE TWO DOGS.

A TALE.

'T was in that place of Scotland's isle
That bears the name of Old King Coil,
Upon a sunny day in June,
When, wearing through the afternoon,
Two dogs did meet, whose random leisure
Had each with other been a pleasure.

The first I 'll name, they called him Cæsar,
Was kept just for his master's pleasure;
His size, his hair, his ears, his head,
Showed he in Scotland ne'er was bred,
But in some island far abroad,
Where sailors go to fish for cod.

His locked and lettered, bright brass collar
Showed him the gentleman and scholar;
But, though he was of high degree,
Was free from pride — no pride had he;
And oft would sport from hour to hour,
Ev'n with a tinker-gipsy cur;
No rusty tyke, black, brown, or yellow,
But found in him a right good fellow,
Who 'd join with them in snuffing, smelling,
And lifting legs, on post or dwelling.

The other was a ploughman's collie,
Owned by a rhymster, ranting, jolly,
Who for his friend and comrade held him,
And in his freaks had Luath called him
After some dog in Highland song,
Made long time since — Lord knows how long.

He was a wise and faithful tyke
As ever leapt o'er ditch or dyke.
His honest, handsome, white-streaked face
Soon found him friends in ev'ry place.
His breast was white, his shaggy back
Well clad in coat of glossy black,
His ample tail, with upward curl,
Hung o'er his haunches with a swirl.

No doubt but each was fond of other,
In very sooth, just like a brother;
With social nose oft snuffed and snifted
For mice and moles, they scratched and rifted;
Sometimes away on long excursion,
Then playful worrying in diversion;
Until with frolic weary grown,
Upon a knoll they sat them down,
And then began a long digression
About the lords of the creation.

CÆSAR.

I've often wondered, honest Luath,
What sort of life poor dogs, like you, have,
And, viewed from life in Palace Hall,
What way poor people lived at all.

My lord gets in his rents and feus,
His coal, his corn, and all his dues;
He rises when he likes, from bed;
His orders brusque, the flunkies dread;
He calls his coach, he calls his horse,
He draws a handsome silken purse
As long's my tail, where through the threads
Are seen the guineas' tails and heads.

From morn till e'en, it's naught but toiling
At baking, roasting, frying, boiling;
The gentry first are stuffed with plenty
The hall folks next get many a dainty
Of dishes fine, that please the taste,
But's little short of downright waste,
Our whipper-in, the blasted sinner,
Poor worthless elf, it eats a dinner
Better than any tenant hand
His honor has in all the land;
And what poor folk put in their bellies
I own it past my power to tell is.

LUATH.

Sometimes, indeed, they're vexed enough;
See that poor cotter, plain and rough,
Digging in ditch, or building dyke,
Working in quarry, and such like;
Himself and wife, and children fair,
He thus sustains, with prudent care;
With toilworn hands he wins their bread,
And keeps a humble roof o'erhead.

And when they meet with sore disasters,
Like loss of health or want of masters,
You most would think, a little longer
And they would starve from cold and hunger,
And why they mostly seem content
Fills me with clear astonishment
Still, stalwart men and clever lasses
Are bred in such a way as this is.

CÆSAR.

But then, to see how you're neglected,
How huffed and cuffed and disrespected;
Lord, man! our gentry care as little
For delvers, ditchers, and such cattle;
They pass them by with nose upturned
As I a swill dish would have spurned.
On rent day, which our lord convenes,
I've noticed sad, pathetic scenes;
Poor tenant folks, of money scant,
Must quietly bear an agent's taunt;

He loudly swears, that, without fail,
He'll seize their goods, send them to jail:
While they must stand, with aspect humble,
And hear it all, and fear and tremble.

I see how folk live that have riches,
But surely poor folk must be wretches.

LUATH.

They're not so wretched's one would think·
Though always on misfortune's brink,
They're so accustomed to the sight
The prospect gives them little fright.

Then chance and fortune are so guided
They're always more or less provided;
And though fatigued with close employment
A blink of rest is sweet enjoyment.

The dearest comfort of their lives
Are thriving children, faithful wives;
The prattling things are just their pride,
That sweetens all their bright fireside.
Sometimes a jug of ale or porter
Will make the longsome hour seem shorter·
They lay aside their private cares,
To mind the Church and State affairs.
They talk of patronage and priests,
With kindling fury in their breasts,
And swear they're by taxation undone,
By these confounded rogues in London.

As bleak-faced Hallowmas returns,
They meet in house or halls or barns,
Where rural life of ev'ry station
Unite in common recreation.
Love blinks, Wit slaps, and social Mirth
Forgets there's care upon the earth.

When New Year leaves the Old behind,
They bar the door on frosty wind;
The social bowl, with mantling ream,
Sends up a heart-inspiring steam;
The reeking pipe and old Scotch snuff
Are handed round, more than enough;
The old folks sitting, talking gladly,
The young folks romping, dancing madly;
Such happiness, without alloy,
Has made me bark, with them, for joy.

Still, it's too true what you have said,
Such game is now too often played.
There's many a creditable stock
Of decent, honest, worthy folk,
Are riven out both root and branch,
Some rascal's prideful greed to quench,
Who thinks to knit himself the faster
In favor with some gentle master,
Who's likely busy parliamenting,
For Britain's good his soul indenting.

CÆSAR.

Ah, lad! you little know about it;
For Britain's good! good faith, I doubt it.
He's like a nag by leaders ridden,
Says aye or no, just when he's bidden·
At operas or plays parading,
Mortgaging, gambling, masquerading;
Or maybe, in a frolic daft,
To Hague or Calais takes a waft,
To make a tour where sin is rife,
Mix with the world, and see high life.

There, at Vienna or Versailles,
He spends his father's old entails·
Or by Madrid consorts with fools
-Who thrum guitars or fight with bulls;
Or down Italian vistas startles,
Wh—re-hunting among groves of myrtles,
Then gulps down bitter German water
To make himself look fair and fatter,
And clear the consequential sorrows,
Love-gifts of Carnival signoras.
For Britain's good!—for her destruction,
With dissipation, feud, and faction!

LUATH.

Cæsar, alas! is that the gait
They run through many a fine estate?
Are we so pinched and sore harassed
For wealth, to go that way at last?

If they would only stay from courts,
And please themselves with country sports
It would for ev'ry one be better,
The squire, the tenant, and the cotter.
Good-hearted, jolly, country squires,
How much in them my heart admires;
Except o'er farms they ride too rudely,
Or of their mistress speaking lewdly
Or shooting of a hare or moorcock,
The ne'er a bit they're ill to poor folk.

But will you tell me, Master Cæsar,
Sure great folks' life's a life of pleasure?
No cold or hunger e'er comes near them,
The very thought need never fear them.

CÆSAR.

Good sir, were you at times where I am,
The wealthy, you would ne'er envy 'em.
It's true they need not starve or sweat,
Through winter's cold or summer's heat;
There's no sore work to craze their bones,
And fill old age with gripes and groans:
But human bodies are such fools,
In spite of colleges and schools,
That when no real ills perplex them,
They make enough themselves to vex them;
And still the less they have to start them,
In like proportion less will hurt them.

A country fellow at the plough,
His acres tilled, care leaves his brow·
A country maiden at her wheel,
Her dozens done, does gladsome feel:
But gentlemen, and ladies worst,
With downright want of work are cursed;
They loiter, lounging, lank and lazy;
Devil bit ails them, yet uneasy;
Their days insipid, dull, and tasteless;
Their nights unquiet, long, and restless;
And e'en their sports, their balls, and races,
Their galloping through public places,
There's such parade, and pomp, and art,
The joy can scarcely reach the heart.

The men fall out in party matches,
Make up again in deep debauches,
At night they're mad with drink and wh——g,
Next day their life is past enduring.

The ladies, arm-in-arm in clusters,
As great and gracious are as sisters;
But hear their absent thoughts of other,
They're devils all, and jades together;
At times, o'er dainty cup and platter,
They sip their tea with scandal clatter,
Or all the night, with crabbed looks,
Pore o'er the devil's pictured books;
Stake on a chance a farmer's stackyard,
And cheat like any unhanged blackguard.
There're some exceptions, man and woman,
But this is gentry's life in common.

By this the sun was out of sight,
And darker gloaming brought the night:
The beetle hummed with lazy drone,
The cows stood lowing in the loan;
When up they got, shook sides, and then
Rejoiced they were but dogs, not men;
And each took off his several way
Resolved to meet some other day.

ADDRESS TO A LOUSE,

ON SEEING ONE ON A LADY'S BONNET IN CHURCH.

Ha! where away, so fast and early,
Your impudence protects you fairly,
I cannot say but you strut rarely
  O'er gauze and lace;
Though faith! I fear you dine but sparely
  On such a place.

You ugly, creeping, blasted runner,
Detested, shunned, by saint and sinner,
How dare you set your foot upon her,
  So fine a lady?
Go somewhere else, and seek your dinner
  On some poor body.

On some poor beggar's head go ramble;
There you may creep, and sprawl, and scramble,
With other kindred, jump and gambol
  In shoals and nations,
Where, undisturbed, you may assemble
  In thick plantations.

Now hold you there! you're out of sight,
Below the ribbons, snug and tight,
No, faith you yet! you'll not be right
  Till you've got on it,
The very topmost, towering height
  Of Miss's bonnet.

It makes me mad to see your nose in
Where folks do wear their finest clothes in.
Oh, for some rank, mercurial rozin,
  Or ointment red,
To see you lie your last death throes in,
  I would be glad.

I'd not have been surprised, mayhap,
To see you on some old wife's cap,
Or head of wee, neglected chap,
        Or coat or vest;
But Miss's leghorn ribbon flap, —
        Get out, you pest!

Dear Jennie, do not toss your head,
And set your beauties all a-spread,
You little know what cursèd speed
        The beast is making, —
Those winks and finger-ends, I dread,
        Are notice taking.

Oh would some power the gift decree us,
To see ourselves as others see us!
It would from many a blunder free us,
        And foolish notion;
What airs in dress and gait would flee us,
        And e'en devotion!

TO A MOUSE,

ON TURNING UP HER NEST WITH THE PLOUGH, NOVEMBER, 1785.

Thou little, sprightly, timorous beast
Why such a panic in thy breast,
You need not start away in haste,
        Or hurrying rustle;
Thy little life I would not waste
        With murd'rous missile.

I'm truly sorry man's dominion
Has broken nature's social union
And justifies that ill opinion
        That makes thee startle
At me, thy poor, earth-born companion,
        And fellow mortal.

At times, I doubt not, thou may thieve,
What then? poor creature, thou must live;
A few small grains from off a sheave
        Are never missed;
A blessing comes, I do believe,
        With all the rest.

Thy fragile house I set my plough in,
The angry wind has left in ruin,
No stuff you'll find to build a new one,—
          There's nothing green;
No place now left to bill and coo in
          In winter keen.

Thou saw the fields laid bare and waste,
And weary winter coming fast,
And cosy here beneath the blast
          Thou thought to dwell,
Till, crash! the cruel plough-share passed
          Out through thy cell.

That little heap of leaves and stubble.
That cost thee many a weary nibble,
You're now bereft, for all thy trouble,
          Of house or hold,
To suffer winter's sleety dribble
          And hoarfrost cold.

But Mousie, not alone us twain
Can prove how foresight may be vain,
The best laid schemes of mice and men
          Go oft awry,
And leave us naught but grief and pain,
          For promised joy.

Still, thou art blest compared with I,
The present only does thee try
But Oh! I look despairingly
          On prospects drear;
The future, which I scarce descry,
          I guess and fear.

ADDRESS TO THE DEVIL.

"O Prince! O Chief of many thronéd Powers,
That led th' embattled Seraphim to war!"
                    —MILTON.

O Thou! whatever title suit thee,
Old Horny, Satan, Nick, or Clootie,
Who in your cavern grim and sooty,
          Close under hatches,
Scatters about the brimstone cootie,
          To scald poor wretches.

Hear me, Old Nick, just for a moment,
And let poor damnèd souls lie dormant;
Small pleasure it must be to torment
          Us weary dogs;
To put us in a torturing ferment,
          And squeal like hogs.

Great is thy power, and great thy fame,
Far known and noted is thy name,
And though yon flaming pit's thy home,
          Wide are your travels;
And faith! you're neither lag nor lame,
          Thou Prince of Devils!

Sometimes like roaring lion hieing,
For prey all holes and corners trying;
At times on strong-winged tempests flying,
          Shaking the spires,
Or lurking in our hearts, outvieing
          Our base desires.

I've heard my reverend granny say,
In lonely glens you like to stray;
Or where old ruined castles gray
          Nod to the moon,
You fright the nightly wand'rer's way,
          Like wizard loon.

When twilight did my granny summon
To say her prayers,—good, honest woman,—
Oft o'er the dyke she's heard you hummin',
          With weirdly drone,
Or rustling through the hedges, coming
          With heavy groan.

One dreary, windy, winter night,
The stars shone down with slanting light,
With you, myself, I got a fright,
          O'er in the mound;
You, like a rash-bush, stood in sight,
          With waving sound.

The cudgel in my hand did shake,
Each bristled hair stood like a stake,
When with a fearful, quaick—quaick—quaick,
          Among the springs,
Away you fluttered like a drake,
          On whistling wings.

Let wizards grim, and withered hags
Tell how, with you, on ragweed nags
They skim the moors and dizzy crags,
      With wicked speed,
And in church-yards renew their leagues
      O'er ravaged dead.

Oft country wives are made your tools;
Obeying customary rules
They churn for butter; but, poor fools
      They fume and fret—
The cows might milkless be as bulls
      For all they get.

Thence mystic knots make great abuse
On fond young husbands, keen and crouse;
When the best work-loom in the house
      Is busy driving;
The merry work is called a truce
      By your contriving.

When thaws dissolve the snowy hoard,
And float the jingling icy board,
The water-kelpies haunt the ford
      At your direction,
And haunted travellers are allured
      To their destruction.

And oft your moss-traversing spunkies
Decoy the wight that late and drunk is;
The blazing, curst, mischievous monkeys
      Delude his eyes,
Till in some miry slough he sunk is
      Ne'er more to rise.

When mason's mystic word and grip
In storms and tempests raise you up,
Some cock or cat your rage must stop,
      Or, strange to tell,
The youngest brother you would whip
      Off straight to hell.

Long since, in Eden's bonny yard,
When youthful lovers first were paired,
And all the soul of love they shared
      The raptured hour,
Sweet on the fragrant, flowery sward,
      In shady bower,

Then you, you wicked, stealthy rogue,
You came to paradise incog.
And with your cursed, insidious brogue
      Caused man to fall,
And gave the infant world a jog,
      'Most ruined all.

One day, when fresh from dark abyss,
— We read it in the Book of Bliss —
You did present your smuttie phiz.
      'Mong better folk,
And scoffed at Job, the man of Uz,
      Your spiteful joke.

Then how you got him in your thrall
And broke him out of house and hall,
While scabs and blotches did him gall
      With scratch and tear,
And, loosed, his wife's ill-humored bawl
      Was worst to bear.

But all your doings to rehearse,
Your wily snares and fighting fierce,
From that day Michael did you pierce,
      Down to this time,
Could not be writ in modern verse,
      Or Runic rhyme.

And now, old Hoofs, I know you're thinking
A certain bard is ranting, drinking,
Some luckless hour will send him linking
      To your black pit;
But faith! he'll turn a corner jinking,
      And cheat you yet.

But, fare you well, old Nickie-ben!
Could you be brought, like sinful men,
To true repentance, you might then
      Still have a stake —
I grieve to think upon yon den,
      E'en for your sake.

TO A MOUNTAIN DAISY,

ON TURNING ONE DOWN WITH THE PLOUGH,
APRIL, 1776.

Sweet, modest flower, with crimson tipped,
The fatal plough has o'er thee slipped,
And thy frail stem untimely ripped
      From Mother Earth;
My hand, unknowing, sure, has nipped
      Thy virgin birth.

Alas! it's not thy neighbor sweet,
The bonny lark, companion meet,
Bending thee 'mong his dewy feet,
      With speckled breast;
When upward springing, glad to greet
      The purpling east.

Cold blew the bitter, biting north
Upon thy early, humble birth,
Yet cheerfully thou ventured forth
      Amid the storm;
Scarce reared above the parent earth,
      Thy tender form.

The flaunting flowers our gardens yield,
High sheltering woods and walls must shield;
But thou, when all else is congealed
      Behind some stone,
Adorns the bleak and barren field,
      Unseen, alone.

There in thy scanty mantle clad,
Thy snowy bosom sunward spread,
Thou lifts thy unassuming head
      In humble guise;
But now the plough uptears thy bed,
      And low thou lies.

Such is the fate of artless maid,
Sweet floweret of the rural shade,
By love's simplicity betrayed,
      And guileless trust,
Till she, like thee, all soiled, is laid
      Low in the dust.

Such is the fate of simple bard,
On life's rough ocean luckless starr'd;
Unskillful he to note the card,
          Of prudent lore,
Till billows rage and gales blow hard,
          And whelm him o'er.

Such fate to suffering worth is given,
Who long with wants and woes has striven,
By human pride or cunning driven
          To misery's brink;
Till wrenched of every stay but heaven,
          He, ruined, sink.

Even thou who mourn'st the daisy's fate,
That fate is thine — no distant date;
Stern Ruin's ploughshare drives elate,
          Full on thy bloom,
Till crushed beneath the furrow's weight
          Shall be thy doom.

DEATH AND DR. HORNBOOK.

[Dr Hornbook is the farcial name the poet gave to a small store-keeper,
who had set up as a self-taught doctor. Burns had met him at a masonic
meeting, on which occasion the apothecary had made some rather con-
ceited brag of his medical lore. The poem followed shortly after, and
had the effect of driving him from the village. He went to Glasgow, and
died there in 1839.]

Some books are lies from end to end,
And some great lies were never penn'd,
Ev'n ministers themselves been kenn'd,
          In holy rapture,
A rousing fib at times to vend,
          And nail 't with Scripture.

But this that I am going to tell,
Which lately on a night befell,
Is just as true 's the Deil's in hell,
          Or Dublin city —
That nearer to us he may dwell,
          The more 's the pity.

The village ale had made me glorious·
I was not full, nor e'en uproarious;
I staggered sometimes, yet victorious
       To free the ditches;
And knew the sound of whistling Boreas
       From drone of witches.

The rising moon began to hover,
The distant Cumnock hills out-over;
To count her horns, with firm endeavor
       Myself I set,
But whether she had three or over,
       I know not yet.

I was come round about the hill,
And tottering down on Willie's mill,
Setting my staff with all my skill,
       I still was ready,
Though sometimes leeward 'gainst my will
       I reeled unsteady.

A something weird then came in sight
That put me in a dreadful fright;
With awful scythe it was bedight
       Upon its shoulder,
While three-pronged dart shone sharp and bright,
       To the beholder.

Its height was far beyond the human,
Its sex seemed neither man nor woman,
It had no atom of abdomen;
       As for it's legs,
They looked as they'd be fine for roamin'
       O'er hills and crags.

Said I, "My friend, have you been mowing
When other folks are busy sowing?"
It seemed to be alert and knowing,
       But nothing spake;
Quoth I, "My friend, where are you going?
       Will you go back?"

It gravely said, "My name is Death,
Be not afraid." Quoth I, "Good faith!
You're maybe come to stop my breath,
       I want no strife —
But warning take, cross not my path,
       See, there's a knife."

"Goodman," said he, "put up your whittle,
I 've no design to try its mettle;
But if I did, I 'd think but little
        To hit you hard,
I do not mind you, not that spittle,
        Out-o'er my beard."

"Well, well!" says I, "it is a bargain;
Give me your hand, we 'll stop this jargon;
Sit down awhile, and here 's some Lurgin,
        Come take a chew:
This flask contains some pleasant gurglin';
        How 's trade with you?"

He paused awhile, and then he said,
"It is a long, long time indeed
Since I began to nick the thread
        And stop the breath;
Folks must do something for their bread,
        And so must Death.

"Six thousand years are near hand fled
Since I was to the butchering bred,
And many a scheme 's in vain been laid
        To scare or stop me,
But one Jock Hornbook's joined the trade
        And may o'er-top me.

"Deil take the paunch of this vile quack
To make a cheap tobacco sack;
He 's got of wondrous cures a knack,
        From scraps he clips,
That boys now mock me at my back,
        And pinch my hips.

"See, here 's a scythe, and there 's a dart,
Have pierced full many a gallant heart,
But Doctor Hornbook, with his art
        And cursèd skill,
Has made them both not worth a ——
        D—d bit they'll kill.

"'T was but last night, at set of sun,
I threw a noble throw at one,—
With less, I 'm sure, have hundred's gone
        To heaven or hell,—
It just played bump against the bone,
        Then useless fell.

"Hornbook was by, with ready art,
And had so fortified the part
That when I looked at my old dart
      It made me savage
To find 't would scarcely pierce the heart
      Of rotten cabbage.

"I drew my scythe in such a fury
I near fell over in my hurry,
But yet the bold apothecary
      Withstood the shock;
I might as well have struck a quarry
      Of granite rock.

"Ev'n them he cannot get attended,
Although their face he never kenn'd it,
Just ——— in cabbage leaf and send it,
      As soon's he smells it,
Both their disease and what will mend it,
      At once he tells it.

He has all kinds of saws and whittles,
All kinds of boxes, mugs, and bottles,
And labelled stuffs, that with the vitals
      Do ill agree;
Their Latin names as fast he rattles
      As A B C.

"Calces of fossils, earths, and trees;
True Sal-marinum of the seas;
The farina of beans and peas,
      He has in plenty;
With Aquafortis, what you please,
      He can content you.

"Besides some new, uncommon weapons,
Urinus spiritus of capons;
Or mitehorn shavings, filings, scrapings,
      Distilled *per se;*
Sal-alkali of midge-tail clippings,
      And more has he.

"Alas, for sexton Johnnie Ged!"
Says I, "if true what you have said,
The churchyard, where the daisies spread
      So white and bonny,
They'll plough up for a cabbage bed ·
      They'll ruin Johnnie."

The creature laughed his loudest pitch;
Says he, "the plough you need not hitch,
Churchyards, the dead will soon enrich,
      You need not fear,
They'll be entrenched in many a ditch
      In two–three year.

"Where one I've fairly killed, in troth
By loss of blood, or breath, or both,
This night I'm free to take my oath,
      That Hornbook's skill
Has clad a score in their last cloth
      By drop and pill.

"An honest weaver to his trade,
Whose wife's two hands were scarce well bred,
Got twopence worth to mend her head
      When it was sore;
She slipped off quietly to her bed
      And ne'er spake more.

"A country squire had got the bots,
Or windy cholic in his guts:
His only son with Hornbook plots
      To breed disaster;
By gift of two small cottage lots,
      He's now the master.

"A bonny lass, you knew her well,
Some ill-brewed drink caused her to swell,
She trusts herself, 'tis sore to tell,
      In Hornbook's care;
She does not hear the tolling bell,
      She's free from care.

"That's just a patch of Hornbook's way;
Thus goes he on from day to day,
Thus does he poison, kill, and slay,
      To my sore hurt,
And cheats me of my lawful prey
      With his d—d dirt.

"But hark! I'll tell you of a plot,
I warn you that you tell it not;
Next time we meet he'll get it hot,
      I wont be sparing;
I'll nail the self-conceited sot
      As dead's a herring!"

He scarce had ceased to vent his spite,
When pealed from out the steeple's height,
Some wee, short hour beyond midnight,
       Which gave us warning:
Death took the road to him was right,
       I homeward turning.

TAM O'SHANTER.

A TALE.

When weary tradesmen leave the street,
And thirsty neighbors, neighbors meet
As market days are wearing past,
And homeward, folks are driving fast;
While we sit happy, feasting, drinking,
With loosened tongues, and eyes a-blinking,
We think not of the long, Scot's miles,
The mosses, waters, dykes, and stiles
That lie between us and our home,
Where sits our sulky, sullen dame,
Gathering her brows like gathering storm,
Nursing her wrath to keep it warm.

This truth, found honest Tam o'Shanter,
As he from Ayr one night did canter;
(Old Ayr, which ne'er a town surpasses,
For honest men and bonny lasses.)

O Tam! had'st thou been shrewd and wise,
To take thy good wife Kate's advice —
And faith! she was not lame nor lazy
To call you drunken, crank, and crazy;
That from November till October,
One market day you ne'er was sober,
And with the miller sit and drink
As long as each had cash to clink;
And ev'ry time the mare was shod,
The smith and you got full's a toad;
That at the village inn on Sunday,
Thou drank with Kirkton Jean till Monday;
She prophesied that, late or soon,
You would be found deep drowned in Doon
Or caught by warlocks or by witches,
Where Alloway's old haunted church is.

Ah, gentle dames! it grieves me sore
How we your counsels do ignore;
How many lengthened, sage advices
The husband from the wife despises!

But to our tale — One market night,
Tam had got planted, snug and right,
Fast by a fire, was blazing finely,
And foaming ale that drank divinely;
There, at his elbow, Souter Johnny,
His ancient, trusty, thirsty crony;
Tam loved him like a very brother,
They had been full for weeks together!
The night drove on with songs and clatter,
And still the ale was growing better..
The landlady and Tam grew gracious
With favors secret, sweet, and precious;
The Souter told his queerest stories;
The landlord's laugh was ready chorus;
The storm without might roar and rustle,
Tam did not mind the storm a whistle.

Care, mad to see such hearty cheer,
E'en drowned himself among the beer!
As bees fly home with loads of treasure,
The minutes winged their way with pleasure;
Kings may be blest, but Tam was glorious,
O'er all the ills of life victorious!
But pleasures are like poppies spread,
You seize the flower, the bloom is shed;
Or like the snowfall on the river,
A moment white, then gone forever;
Or like the borealis race
That flit e'er you can point their place;
Or like the rainbow's lovely form
Evanishing amid the storm.
But for no man waits time or tide;
The hour approaches, Tam must ride,—
That hour, of night's black arch the keystone,
When he must mount his faithful beast on;
And such a night he takes the road in,
As ne'er poor sinner was abroad in.

The wind blew as 't would blow its last,
The rattling showers rose on the blast,
The lightning gleams the darkness swallowed,
Loud, deep, and long, the thunder bellowed;
That night, a child might understand
The Deil had business on his hand.

Well-mounted on his gray mare, Meg,
A better never lifted leg,
Tam spattered on through mud and mire,
Despising wind and rain and fire;
Now holding fast his broad blue bonnet,
And humming o'er some old Scot's sonnet,
Or peering round with prudent care,
Lest witches catch him unaware
Kirk Alloway was drawing nigh,
Where ghosts and owls make nightly cry.

The ford was reached, and elm tree withered,
Near where the snow the pedler smothered;
Then passed the place and saw the rock
Where drunken Charlie's neck was broke;
And through the moorland, bleak and wild,
Where hunters found the murdered child;
Then neared the thorn and rocky shelf
Where Mungo's mother hanged herself.
Before him Doon pours all his floods,
The doubling storm roars through the woods;
The lightnings flash from pole to pole;
Loud, and more loud the thunders roll;
When, glimmering through the murky haze,
Kirk Alloway seemed in a blaze;
From doors and windows lights were glancing,
And loud resounded mirth and dancing.

Inspiring, bold John Barleycorn,
What dangers thou can'st make us scorn!
With home-brewed ale we fear no evil,
With whiskey straight, we'll face the Devil.
The drink so reamed in Tammie's head,
Fair play, the devils he defied;
But Maggie stood right sore astonished
Till by the heel and hand admonished
She ventured forward on the light,
And Oh! Tam saw an awful sight;
Warlocks and witches in a dance;
No fine cotillions new from France,
But hornpipes, jigs, strathspeys, and reels,
Put life and mettle in their heels:
On window sill, sat in the east,
Old Nick himself, in shape of beast,—
A hairy creature, black and large,—
To give them music was his charge;
He squeezed the pipes and made them scream,
That echoed loud from roof and beam.

Uncovered coffins stood in rows,
Which showed the dead in their last clothes
And by some devilish spell of night
Each in his cold hand held a light,
By which heroic Tam was able
To note upon the holy table
A gibbet, where a murderer grins;
Two span-long, wee, unchristened twins;
A thief, just from a rope cut down,
Upon his face an awful frown;
Five tomahawks, with blood red-rusted;
Five scimitars, with murder crusted;
A cord, by which a babe was strangled;
A knife, a father's throat had mangled,
Whose son had him bereft of life,
The gray hairs yet stuck to the knife·
With more of horrible and awful,
Which even to name, would be unlawful.

As Tammie stared, amazed and curious,
The mirth and fun grew fast and furious
The piper loud and louder blew,
The dancers quick and quicker flew;
They reeled like mad, they crossed, they set,
Till, fairly crazed with reeking sweat,
They cast their clothes, the naughty flirts,
And lilted at it in their shirts.

Now Tam! O Tam! had they been queens,
All plump and strapping, in their teens,
Their shirts, instead of flannel greasy,
Had been of muslin, thin and sleazy;
Those breeches mine (my only pair),
That once were plush, of good blue hair,
I'd given them freely off my haunches
For one sight of the bonny wenches:

But withered hags, sly and insidious,
Unhanged old beldams, swarth and hideous,
Capering and floundering o'er a broomstick,
I wonder did not make thee homesick.

But Tam knew what was what full well;
There was one bright and winsome belle
That night enlisted in the core,
(Long after known on Carrick shore;

For many a beast to death she shot,
And perish'd many a bonny boat,
And shook the corn in stock and ear,
And kept the country side in fear.)
Her cutty shirt of Paisley yarn,
That, while a lassie, she had worn
Its longitude though sorely scanty,
Pleased Tam the most, he thought 't was plenty.

Ah! little knew thy reverend granny
That shirt she bought for her wee Nanny,
With two pounds Scots ('t was all her riches)
Would ever grace a dance of witches.

But here my Muse her wing must lower,
Such flights are far beyond her power;
To sing how Nanny sprang and lept
(A supple jade and well adept),
And how Tam stood with eyes bewitched
And thought his very eyes enriched;
Old Nick, himself, grew fond and fain,
And shugged and blew with might and main
Till first one caper, then another
Tam lost his reason altogether.
When, " Well done, Cutty shirt!" he bellowed,—
Thick darkness closed the scene unhallowed·
And scarcely had he Maggie rallied,
When out the hellish legion sallied.
As bees rush out with angry fuss,
When plundering herds assail their house;
Or hare, pursued by mortal foes,
When pop! she starts before their nose;
As eager runs the market crowd,
When "catch the thief!" resounds aloud;
So Maggie runs, the witches follow,
With most unearthly screech and holla.

Oh, Tam! beware thy fate unerring,
In hell they'll roast thee like a herring!
In vain thy Kate awaits thy comin'!
Kate soon will be a woeful woman!
Now Meg, stretch every shank and shin,
The keystone of the bridge to win;
There at them thou thy tail may toss,
A running stream they dare not cross;
But ere the keystone she could make,
The ne'er a tail she had to shake;

For Nannie, far before the rest,
Hard upon noble Maggie pressed,
And flew at Tam, his case to settle;
But little wist she Maggie's mettle —
One spring brought off her master hale,
But left behind her own gray tail;
For Nan had caught her by the rump,
And left poor Maggie scarce a stump.

Now who this tale of truth shall read,
Each man and mother's son take heed·
Whene'er to drink you are inclined,
Or cutty shirts run in your mind,
Of such illusive joys beware,
Remember Tam o' Shanter's mare.

ADDRESS TO THE EXTRA GOOD, OR RIGIDLY RIGHTEOUS.

" My son, these maxims make a rule,
  And lump them all together:
The rigid righteous is a fool,
  The rigid wise another;
The cleanest corn, on closer sight,
  May have some grains suspicious;
So ne'er a fellow creature slight,
  Though sometimes, injudicious. "
                    — SOLOMON — Eccles. vii. 16.

O you who think yourselves so great,
  So pious and so holy,
And who incessantly dilate
  On neighbors' faults and folly,
Your tongue is like a fast-run mill
  Supplied with store of water,
The heaped-up hopper's ebbing still,
  And still the clap plays clatter.

Hear me, ye venerable core,
  As counsel for poor mortals
That frequently pass Wisdom's door,
  For thoughtless Folly's portals;
I, for their weak and heedless sakes
  Would here propose defences,
Their careless tricks, their black mistakes
  Their failings and mischances.

You see your state with theirs compared,
  With hypocritic sufferance :
But cast a moment's fair regard,
  What makes the mighty difference ?
Discount your lack of fervent zest.
  That purity you pride in,
And oft, — what's more than all the rest,—
  Your better art of hiding.

Think, when your conscience-stricken pulse
  Gives now and then a wallop,
What raging must his veins convulse
  That still eternal gallop.
With wind and tide fair at your tail,
  Right on you scud your sea-way
But in the teeth of both to sail,
  It makes a dreadful leeway.

See social life and glee sit down,
  All joyous and unthinking,
Till metamorphosed they have grown,
  With deep debauch and drinking.
Oh would they stay to calculate,
  Th' eternal consequences ;
Or your more dreaded hell to state,
  Damnation of expenses.

Ye high, exalted, virtuous dames
  Tied up in godly laces,
Before you give poor frailty names
  Suppose a change of cases ;
A dear loved lad, convenience near
  A treacherous inclination —
But, let me whisper in your ear,
  Perhaps you're no temptation.

Then gently scan your brother man,
  Still gentler sister woman ;
Though error's road they may have ran,
  To step aside is human :
One point must still be greatly dark
  The question why they do it :
And just as lamely can we mark
  How far perhaps they rue it.

Who made the heart, 'tis He alone
  Decidedly can try us;
He knows each chord — its various tone,
  Each spring — its various bias:
Then at the balance let's be mute
  We never can adjust it;
What's done, we partly may compute,
  But know not what's resisted.

LINES ON MEETING WITH LORD DAER.

This note you all whom it concerns,
I, Rhymer Robin, alias Burns,
    October twenty-third,
A ne'er-to-be-forgotten day!
When, after climbing up the way,
    I dinnered with a lord.

I've been at drunken lawyers' feasts,
Nay, been blind full with godly priests,
    With reverence I speak it;
I've even joined the honored jorum
When mighty squireships of the quorum
    Their hydra thirst did slake it.

But with a lord — stand out, my shin!
A lord — a peer — an earl's son! —
    Up higher yet, my bonnet!
And such a lord, o'er six feet tall! —
Our peerage, he o'erlooks them all
    As I look o'er my sonnet.

But, oh! for Hogarth's magic rare,
To show the Bard's dumbfounded stare,
    And how he hemmed and stammered!
When moving as if led by noose,
And stumping in his ploughman shoes
    He in the parlor hammered.

To meet good Stewart little pain is
Or Scotia's sacred Demosthenes;
    Thinks I, they are but human,
But Burns, my lord — my heart was quaking,
I plainly felt my knees were shaking,
    And weak as any woman.

I sidling sheltered in a nook,
And at his lordship stole a look,
    Like some portentous omen;
Except good sense and social glee,
And — what surprised me — modesty,
    I nothing saw uncommon.

I watched for symptoms of the great,
The gentle pride, the lordly state,
    The arrogant assuming;
He showed no pride, no pride had he,
Nor lofty state, that I could see,
    More than an honest ploughman.

Then from his lordship I shall learn,
Henceforth to meet with unconcern
    One rank as well's another.
No honest, worthy man need care
To meet with noble, youthful Daer,
    For he but meets a brother.

VERSES ON A SCOTCH BARD

GONE TO THE WEST INDIES.

[Written at the time he thought of going to the West Indies.]

All you who live by sups of drink,
All you who make the verses clink
All you who live but never think
    Come mourn with me;
Our Bard, of all the Bards the pink
    Is o'er the sea.

Lament him all ye merry band,
Who oft have felt his magic wand;
No more he'll join you hand in hand,
    In social key;
For now he's left his native strand,
    And o'er the sea.

The bonny lasses well may praise him,
And in their dear petitions place him;
The widows, wives, and all may bless him,
    And pleasures flee;
For well I wot, they'll sorely miss him
    That's o'er the sea.

O Fortune! they might well complain!
Had'st thou removed some drowsy swain,
Some soulless knave who lives in vain,
        They had no plea;
But he could cheer them with his strain,
        That's o'er the sea.

Old Kyle may mourning garments wear,
And stain them with the salt, salt tear;
'Twill make her poor old heart, I fear,
        In flinders flee;
He was her Laureate many a year,
        That's o'er the sea.

He saw life's sky was overcast,
Long mustering up a bitter blast;
Misfortune broke his heart at last,
        Ill may she be!
So, took a berth before the mast,
        And o'er the sea.

He long with Fate had fought a duel,
On scarce a stomachful of gruel;
His spirit proud, with lot so cruel
        Could ill agree;
A hammock bore this precious jewel
        Out o'er the sea.

He was not given to great misguiding,
Yet coin his pockets would not bide in;
With him it ne'er was under hiding,
        He dealt it free;
The Muse was all that he took pride in,
        That's o'er the sea.

Jamaica bodies, do your best,
And help him to a cosy nest;
The motions that inspire his breast
        Are full of glee;
He would not wrong hell's blackest pest,
        That's o'er the sea.

Farewell, our rhyme-composing brother!
In native soil your root did wither;
But may you flourish like the heather,
        Now, bright and free;
We'll toast you, one and all, together,
        Though o'er the sea.

THE COTTER'S SATURDAY NIGHT.

Let not ambition mock their useful toil,
Their homely joys, and destiny obscure;
Nor grandeur hear with a disdainful smile,
The short but simple annals of the poor.— GRAY.

My loved, my honored, much-respected friend!
  No mercenary bard his homage pays;
With honest pride, I scorn each selfish end,
  My dearest meed, a friend's esteem and praise:
To you I sing, in simple Scottish lays,
  The lowly train in life's sequester'd scene;
The native feelings strong, the guileless ways;
  What Aiken in a cottage would have been;
Ah! tho' his worth unknown, far happier there, I ween!

November chill blows through the leafless bough;
  The short'ning winter day is near a close;
The miry beasts retreating from the plough;
  The black'ning trains of crows to their repose;
The toil-worn cotter from his labor goes,
  This night his weekly toil is at an end,
Collects his spades, his mattocks, and his hoes,
  Hoping the morn in ease and rest to spend,
And weary o'er the moor his course does homeward
      bend.

And when his lonely cot he nears unto,
  Beneath the shelter of an aged tree,
Th' expectant children, when he comes in view,
  Run out to meet their dad, with gladsome noise
      and glee.
His welcome fireside, blinking bonnily,
  His clean hearthstone, his thrifty wife's sweet smile,
The lisping infant prattling on his knee,
  Does all his weary, cank'ring cares beguile,
And makes him quite forget his labors and his toil.

Betimes, the older ones come dropping in,
  Who are at service 'mong the farmer neighbors;
One holds the plough, some herd, and others win
  A pittance small, by sundry jobs and labors·
Their oldest hope, their Jenny, woman grown,
  In youthful bloom, so charming for to see,
Comes home, perhaps to show a fine new gown,
  Or freely give her sore-won penny fee
To help her parents dear, if they in hardship be.

With joy unfeigned, brothers and sisters meet,
   And each for other's welfare kind enquire;
The social hours, swift-winged, unnoticed fleet
   In tales of dreadful news by flood and fire;
The parents, partial, eye their hopeful years;
   Anticipation forward points the view.
The mother, with her needle and her shears,
   Makes old clothes look almost as well as new;
The father mixes all with admonition due.

Their master's and their mistress's command,
   The youngsters all are cautioned to obey;
And mind their labors with a careful hand,
   And ne'er, though out of sight, to idly play;
"And oh! be sure to fear the Lord alway!
   And mind your duty, duly, morn and night!
Lest in temptation's path ye walk astray,
   Implore his counsel and assisting might;
They never sought in vain that sought the Lord
    aright!"

But hark! a rap comes gently to the door;
   Jenny, who knows the meaning of the same,
Tells how a neighbor lad came o'er the moor
   To do some errands, and convoy her home.
The wily mother sees the conscious flame
   Sparkle in Jenny's eye, and flush her cheek;
With heart-struck, anxious care, inquires his name,
   Which Jenny halfway is afraid to speak;
Well pleased the mother hears it's no wild, worthless
    rake.

With kindly words, he's further welcom'd in,—
   A strapping youth; he takes the mother's eye;
The father's favor he at once does win;
   They talk of horses, ploughs, and wheat and rye;
The youngster's artless heart o'erflows with joy;
   Yet still the scene his courage puts to test;
The mother, with a woman's wiles, can spy
   What makes the youth so bashfully distressed;
Well pleased to think her child's respected like the
    rest.

    .   .   .   .

But now the supper crowns the simple board,
   The wholesome porridge, chief of Scotia's food;
With good, sweet milk, the cow can well afford,
   That in the barn so quietly chews her cud.

The dame, who feels in complimental mood,
  Brings in her cheese, so rich in taste and smell,
And oft he's pressed, and oft he calls it good;
  The frugal wife, so garrulous, will tell
How 'twas a twelvemonth old, when lint was in
    the bell.

The cheerful supper done, with serious face,
  They round the fireside form a circle wide·
The sire turns o'er, with patriarchal grace,
  The big hall Bible, once his father's pride;
His bonnet rev'rently is laid aside,
  That shows his old gray locks, so thin and bare;
Those strains that once did sweet in Zion glide,
  Of which a portion he selects with care,
And "Let us worship God," he says, with solemn
  · air.

They chant their artless notes in simple guise;
  They tune their hearts, by far the noblest aim;
Perhaps "Dundee's" wild warbling measures rise,
  Or plaintive "Martyrs," worthy of the name·
Or noble "Elgin" fans the heavenward flame,
  The sweetest far of Scotia's holy lays:
Compared with these, Italian trills are tame;
  The tickled ear no heartfelt raptures raise,
No unison have they with our Creator's praise.

The priest-like father reads the sacred page,
  How Abram was the friend of God on high·
Or Moses bade eternal warfare wage
  With Amalek's ungracious progeny;
Or how the royal bard did groaning lie
  Beneath the stroke of Heaven's avenging ire;
Or Job's pathetic plaint, and wailing cry;
  Or rapt Isaiah's wild seraphic fire;
Or other holy seers that tune the sacred lyre.

Perhaps the Christian volume is the theme,
  How guiltless blood for guilty man was shed;
How HE, who bore in heaven the second name,
  Had not on earth whereon to lay His head!
How His first followers and servants sped;
  The precepts sage they wrote to many a land:
How he, who lone in Patmos banishèd,
  Saw in the sun a mighty angel stand;
And heard great Bab'lon's doom pronounced by
    Heaven's command.

Then, kneeling down, to HEAVEN's ETERNAL KING,
  The saint, the father, and the husband prays:
Hope "springs exulting on triumphant wing,"
  That thus they all shall meet in future days;
There, ever bask in uncreated rays,
  No more to sigh or shed the bitter tear,
Together hymning their Creator's praise,
  In such society, yet still more dear;
While circling time moves round in an eternal
    sphere.

Compared with this, how poor religion's pride,
  In all the pomp of method, and of art,
When men display to congregations wide
  Devotion's every grace, except the heart!
The Power, incensed, the pageant will desert,
  The pompous strain, the sacerdotal stole;
But haply, in some cottage far apart,
  May hear, well pleased, the language of the soul,
And in his Book of Life the inmates poor enrol.

Then homeward all take off their several way;
  The youngling cottagers retire to rest;
The parent-pair their secret homage pay,
  And proffer up to heaven the warm request,
That HE who stills the raven's clam'rous nest,
  And decks the lily fair in flow'ry pride,
Would, in the way his wisdom sees the best,
  For them and for their little ones provide,
But chiefly in their hearts with grace divine preside.

From scenes like these old Scotia's grandeur springs,
  That makes her loved at home, revered abroad;
Princes and lords are but the breath of kings,
  "An honest man 's the noblest work of GOD;"
And certes, in fair virtue's heav'nly road,
  The cottage leaves the palace far behind.
What is a lordling's pomp?—a cumbrous load,
  Disguising oft the wretch of humankind,
Studied in arts of hell, in wickedness refined!

O Scotia! my dear, my native soil!
  For whom my warmest wish to Heav'n is sent,
Long may thy hardy sons of rustic toil
  Be blest with health, and peace, and sweet content!
And, oh! may Heaven their simple lives prevent
  From luxury's contagion, weak and vile!

Then, howe'er crowns and coronets be rent,
  A virtuous populace may rise the while,
And stand a wall of fire around their much-loved
    isle.

O Thou! who pour'd the patriotic tide
  That stream'd thro' Wallace's undaunted heart,
Who dared to nobly stem tyrannic pride,
  Or nobly die, the second glorious part;
(The patriot's God, peculiarly thou art,
  His friend, inspirer, guardian, and reward!)
Oh never, never, Scotia's realm desert;
  But still the patriot, and the patriot-bard,
In bright succession raise, her ornament and guard!

———

❦ THE JOLLY BEGGARS.

[Sir Walter Scott, his son-in-law Lockhart, and Allan Cunningham, were extravagant in their praise of this lyrical drama of low life. Burns, and one or two of his friends were present in " Poosie Nancy's " at an uproarious gathering of beggars and tinkers; the result of which was the famous cantata.]

When withered leaves bestrew the ground,
Or like the bats when flitting round,
  Bedim cold Boreas' blast;
When hail-stones drive with bitter pelt,
And infant frosts again are felt,
  In filmy whiteness drest;
On such a night, a merry set
  Of mongrel loons and vagrant,
In Poosie Nancy's snug had met,
  Mid stenches most unfragrant,
    With quaffing and laughing,
      They ranted and they sang;
    With jumping and thumping,
      The very griddle rang.

First, next the fire, in old red rags,
One sat, well braced with mealy bags,
  And knapsack all in order;
His doxy lay within his arm,
With whiskey strong, and blankets warm —
  She fondly eyed her sodger;
And still he gave the frouzy drab,
  The other rousing kiss,

While she held up her greedy gab,
  With lusty amorousness.
    Each smack still, did crack still,
      Just like a pedler's whip;
    Then staggering and swaggering,
      He roared this ditty up —

AIR.

TUNE — "*Soldier's Joy.*"

I am a son of Mars, who have been in many wars
And show my cuts and scars wherever I come;
This here was for a wench, and that other in a
      trench,
When welcoming the French at the sound of the
      drum.
                    Lal de daudle, etc.

My 'prenticeship I passed where my leader breath'd
      his last,
When the bloody die is cast on the heights of
      Abram;
I served out my trade when the gallant game was
      play'd,
And the Moro low was laid at the sound of the
      drum.
                    Lal de daudle, etc.

I lastly was with Curtis, among the floating batt'ries,
And there I left for witness an arm and a limb;
Yet let my country need me, with Elliot to head me,
I'd clatter on my stumps at the sound of a drum.
                    Lal de daudle, etc.

And now, though I must beg, with a wooden arm
      and leg,
And many a tatter'd rag hanging over my bum,
I'm as happy with my wallet, my bottle, and my
      callet,
As when I us'd in scarlet to follow a drum.
                    Lal de daudle, etc.

What tho' with hoary locks, I must stand the winter
      shocks,
Beneath the woods and rocks oftentimes for a home,

When the t'other bag I sell, and the t'other bottle
   tell,¹
I could meet a troop of hell at the sound of a
   drum.
Lal de daudle, etc.

   He ended, and the rafter shook
     Above the chorus roar;
   While frightened rats, with backward look,
     Seek out the inmost bore;
   A fairy fiddler from the nook,
     He loudly yelled " Encore ! "
 • But up arose the martial chuck,
     And laid the loud uproar —

AIR.

TUNE — " Soldier Laddie. "

I once was a maid, though I cannot tell when,
And still my delight is in proper young men;
Some one of a troop of dragoons was my daddie,
No wonder I'm fond of a sodger laddie.
   Sing, Lal de lal, etc.

The first of my loves was a swaggering blade,
To rattle the thundering drum was his trade;
His leg was so tight, and his cheek was so ruddy,
Transported I was with my sodger laddie.
   Sing, Lal de lal, etc.

But the godly old chaplain left him in the lurch;
The sword I forsook for the sake of the church;
He ventured the soul, and I risked the body,
'T was then I proved false to my sodger laddie.
   Sing, Lal de lal, etc.

Full soon I grew sick of my sanctified sot,
The regiment at large for a husband I got;
From the gilded spontoon to the fife I was ready,
I asked no more but a sodger laddie.
   Sing, Lal de lal, etc.

But the peace it reduced me to beg in despair,
Till I met my old boy at a Cunningham fair;
His rags regimental they flutter'd so gaudy
My heart it rejoiced at a sodger laddie.
        Sing, Lal de lal, etc.

And now I have lived — I know not how long,
And still I can join in a cup or a song·
But whilst with both hands I can hold the glass
    steady,
Here's to thee, my hero, my sodger laddie.
        Sing, Lal de lal, etc.

Poor, merry Andrew in the nook,
  Sat guzzling with a tinker huzzy,
No part they in the chorus took,
  Between themselves they were so busy·
At length with drink and courting dizzy,
  He staggered up and made a face,
Then turned and laid a smack on Grizzie,
  And tuned his pipes with grave grimace —

AIR.

TUNE — "*Old Sir Simon.*"

Sir Wisdom's a fool when he's drunk,
  Sir Knave is a fool in a session;
But there he's a novice, I think,
  While I am a fool by profession.

My granny, she bought me a book
  And I held away to the school;
I fear I my talent mistook,
  But what will you have of a fool?

For drink I would venture my neck;
  A wench is the half of my craft;
But what would you other expect
  Of one who's avowedly daft.

I once was tied up like a steer
  For civilly swearing and laughing;
I once was abused far and near
  For romping with lasses, and chaffing.

Poor Andrew, that tumbles for sport,
  Let nobody name with a jeer;
There's even, I'm told, in the court
  A tumbler they call the Premier.

Observe ye yon reverend cad
  Make faces to tickle the mob?
He rails at our mountebank squad —
  It's rivalship just in the job.

To conclude, I've no riches nor pelf,
  But faith, I'm confoundedly dry;
And the man that's a fool for himself,
  Good Lord! he's far dafter than I.

Then next outspoke a rough old beldam,
Who had been dipped in wells, not seldom ·
For many a purse and many a locket
By her was filched from many a pocket.
Her dove, one of those Highland fellows,
Had died upon the hangman's gallows;
With sighs and sobs she thus began
To wail her handsome Highlandman: —

AIR.

Tune — *White Cockade.*

A Highland lad my love was born,
The Lowland laws he held in scorn;
But he still was faithful to his clan,
My gallant, brave John Highlandman.

CHORUS.

Sing, hey, my brave John Highlandman!
Sing, ho, my brave John Highlandman!
There's not a lad in all the clan
Could match my brave John Highlandman.

With his philabeg and tartan plaid,
And good claymore down by his side,
The ladies' hearts he did trepan, —
My gallant, brave John Highlandman
    CHORUS — Sing, hey, etc.

We ranged from Tweed to Forth and Spey,
And lived like lords and ladies gay;
For a Lowland face he feared not one,—
My gallant, brave John Highlandman.
        CHORUS — Sing, hey, etc.

They banished him beyond the sea;
But ere the bud was on the tree,
Adown my cheeks the pearls ran,
Embracing my John Highlandman.
        CHORUS — Sing, hey, etc.

But, oh! they catched him at the last,
And bound him in a dungeon fast:
My curse upon them, every one;
They've hanged my brave John Highlandman.
        CHORUS — Sing, hey, etc.

And now a widow, I must mourn
The pleasures that will ne'er return :
No comfort but a hearty can
Can cheer me for my Highlandman.
        CHORUS — Sing, hey, etc.

———

A pigmy chap then up did sidle,
Who used at fairs to scrape and fiddle;
Her strapping limb and bouncing middle
        (He reached no higher),
Had holed his heart through like a riddle,
        And set on fire.

Inspired by love and Eau de vie,
He tuned his gamut, one, two, three;
Then, in an arioso key,
        The wee Apollo
Set off, with allegretto glee,
        His giga solo.

———

AIR.

TUNE — *Whistle o'er the lave o't.*

Let me reach up to wipe that tear,
And go with me and be my dear,
And then your ev'ry care and fear
        May whistle th' remainder.

CHORUS.

I am a fiddler to my trade,
And all the tunes that e'er I played,
The sweetest still to wife or maid,
Was whistle th' remainder.

At dance or wedding we 'll be there,
And oh ! so nicely 's we will fare;
We 'll bouse about till Daddy Care
  Sings whistle th' remainder.
          CHORUS — I am, etc.

With bones to pick, and bread and cheese,
In sunny nooks we 'll take our ease,
And at our leisure, when you please,
  We 'll whistle th' remainder.
          CHORUS — I am, etc.

And while your charms such comfort brings,
And while I tickle hair on strings,
Hunger, cold, and all such things
  May whistle th' remainder.
          CHORUS — I am, etc.

———

A tinker bold her charms had shared,
  As well as poor gut-scraper;
He takes the fiddler by the beard
  And draws a rusty rapier.

He swore by all was swearing worth
  To spear his lights and liver,
Unless he would, from that time forth,
  Relinquish her forever.

With trembling knee, poor tweedle-dee
  Upon his haunches bended,
And prayed for grace, with rueful face,
  And so the quarrel ended

But though his little heart did grieve
  When round the tinker pressed her,
He feigned to snicker in his sleeve
  When thus her knight addressed her : —

AIR.

Tune — *Clout the Cauldron.*

My bonny lass, I work in brass,
  A tinker is my station;
I 've travelled round all Christian ground
  In this, my occupation.
I've ta'en the gold, and been enrolled
  In many a noble squadron;
But vain they searched, when off I marched
  To go and clout the cauldron.

Despise that shrimp, that withered imp,
  With all his noise and caperin',
And take a share with those that bear
  The budget and the apron.
Then be my lass, and by this glass
  Of smuggled stuff so handy,
If you e'er want, or come to scant,
  May I ne'er taste this brandy.

————

His suit prevailed — the unblushing fair
  In his embraces sunk;
Partly o'ercome by love's ensnare
  And partly she was drunk.
Sir Violino, with an air
  That showed a man of spunk,
Wished unison between the pair,
  And made the bottle clunk
        To their health that night.

But Cupid shot a dame a shaft,
  That hit her fair and square;
The fiddler raked her fore and aft,
  Behind the chicken lair.
Her lord, a wight of Homer's craft,
  Though spavined as a mare,
Got up and danced and screech'd and laugh'd,
  And sang a lusty air
        To boot, that night.

He was a care-defying blade
  As ever Bacchus listed;
Though Fortune sore upon him laid,
  His heart, she ever missed it.

He had no wish but — to be glad,
No want but — when he thirsted;
He hated nought but — to be sad,
And thus the muse suggested
His song that night.

———

AIR.

TUNE — *For a' that and a' that.*

I am a bard of small regard
With gentle folks, and all that;
But Homer-like, around the dyke,
To gaping crowds I bawl that.

CHORUS.

For all that, and all that,
And twice as much as all that;
I 've one to find, I 've two behind,
I 've wife enough for all that.

I never drank the Muse's tank,
Castalia's brook, and all that;
But there it streams, and richly reams,
My Helicon I call that.
CHORUS — For all that, etc.

Great love I bear to all the fair,
Their humble slave, and all that;
But lordly will I hold it still
A mortal sin to gall that.
CHORUS — For all that, etc.

In raptures sweet this hour we meet
With mutual love, and all that;
So, on this night the flea may bite
As long's it does not pall that.
CHORUS — For all that, etc.

Their tricks and craft have made me daft,
They've ta'en me in, and all that;
But clear your decks, and here's the sex,
I like the jades for all that.

CHORUS.

For all that, and all that,
  And twice as much as all that;
My dearest blood, to do them good,
  They're welcome still for all that.

———

He ended—and from Nancy's walls
The loud applause and blatant yells
    Re-echoed from each mouth;
They shook their bags, and pawned their duds
Till nearly nude, but what's the odds
    Against oppressive drouth?
Then o'er again, the jovial throng
    The poet did request
To loose his pack, and choose a song,
    A ballad of the best.
      He, rising, rejoicing,
        Between his two Deborahs,
  Looks round him, and found them
      Impatient for the chorus.

———

AIR.

TUNE—*Jolly Mortals, Fill Your Glasses.*

See the smoking bowl before us!
  Mark our jovial, ragged ring!
Round and round take up the chorus,
  And in raptures let us sing.

CHORUS.

A fig for those by law protected!
  Liberty's a glorious feast!
Courts for cowards were erected,
  Churches built to please the priest.

What is title? what is treasure?
  What is reputation's care?
If we lead a life of pleasure,
  'T is no matter how or where.
              A fig, etc.

With the ready trick and fable,
  Round we wander all the day;
And at night, in barn or stable,
  Hug our doxies on the hay.
              A fig, etc.

Does the train-attended carriage
  Thro' the country lighter rove?
Does the sober bed of marriage
  Witness brighter scenes of love?
              A fig, etc.

Life is all a *variorum*,
  We regard not how it goes;
Let them cant about decorum
  Who have characters to lose.
              A fig, etc.

Here's to budgets, bags, and wallets!
  Here's to all the wand'ring train!
Here's our ragged brats and callets!
  One and all cry out, Amen!

A fig for those by law protected!
  Liberty's a glorious feast!
Courts for cowards were erected,
  Churches built to please the priest.

THE TARBOLTON LASSES.

Fair Peggy lives on yon hill-top,
  A girl both bright and ready ·
She knows her father is a lord,
  And knows that she's a lady.

At Sophie dear, you need not jeer,—
  She has a handsome fortune;
Who cannot win her in a night
  Has little art in courtin'.

Go down by Faile and taste the ale,
  And take a look at Mysie.
She is a stubborn, wilful jade,
  Yet still she might entice ye.

If she be shy, her sister try;
  You 'll maybe fancy Jenny,
If you 'll dispense with want of sense,
  She knows herself she 's bonny.

And when you climb up yon hillside,
  Just ask for bonny Bessie;
She will invite you to alight
  And handsomely address ye.

There 're few so pretty, none so good
  In all the king's dominion,—
Whatever *you* may think of this
  'T is Bessie's own opinion.

LASSES OF TARBOLTON.

Tarbolton, I ween, has proper young men,
  And proper young women beside, man;
But know that the Ronalds, that live in the Bennals,
  They ride on the top of the tide, man.

Their father 's a lord, and well can afford
  Good money to dower them all, man;
To a proper young man, he 'll clink in his hand
  A sum neither stingy nor small, man.

There 's one that 's called Jean, I warrant you 've seen
  As handsome a lass and as tall, man;
But for sense and good taste, she 'll vie with the best,
  And a conduct that beautifies all, man.

The charms of the mind, the longer you 'll find,
  The more admiration they draw, man,
While roses and lilies on cheeks of young fillys
  Are oft seen on the lass that is raw, man.

If you 're after Miss Jean (on my word you can lean),
  You have rivals that you never saw, man;
The lord of Blackbyre would walk through the fire,—
  Could he wed her according to law, man.

The lord of Braehead has been on his speed
  To win her fair hand in his paw, man;
The lord of the Ford will be stretched on a board,
  If his hopes they should chance for to yaw, man.

Then Anna comes in, the pride of her kin,
  With a heart that has never a flaw, man;
Of her modesty sweet, and sense so complete,
  The bachelors ne'er cease to jaw, man.

If my mind was confessed as to which was the best
  Of the lasses that ever I saw, man,
The fault would be mine if she did not shine
  Over all, like the snow on Skiddaw, man.

I'd woo her myself, if I only had pelf,
  But poverty keeps me in awe, man;
For making of rhymes, and working at times,
  ,Brings but little cash in the claw, man.

Yet I would not choose to let her refuse,
  Or hear the word no from her maw, man;
For though I am poor, unnoticed, obscure,
  I am proud as an eastern pasha, man.

Though I cannot ride in well-booted pride,
  And flee o'er the hills like a crow, man,
I can hold up my head with the best of the breed,
  Though I handle the spade and the hoe, man.

My coat and my vest, they are Scotch of the best,
  Of pairs of good breeches, I've two, man,
And stockings and pumps to put on my stumps,
  And ne'er a wrong stitch peeping through, man.

My shirts they are few, but five of them new,
  All linen as white as the snow, man,
A ten shilling hat, a Holland cravat,
  Thing of which but few poets can blow, man.

I never had friends with wealth or stipends,
  To leave me a few hundred pounds, man;
Nor aunties with riches to wish the old witches
  Were snugly laid under the mounds, man.

I ne'er had the gift of hoarding or thrift,
  I never did make a great show, man
I've little to spend, and nothing to lend,
  But devil a shilling I owe, man.

HOLY WILLIE'S PRAYER.

An "eXquisitely severe satire" was the language of Sir Walter Scott in regard to this poem. The hero, William Fisher, was an officious and hypocritical elder of Mr. Auld's church. Burns' animosity was roused against him, owing to the rancor with which he persecuted his friend, Gavin Hamilton, for some trivial offence of work done in his garden on Sunday by a poor itinerant. As a result, Hamilton was put under the ban of the church. Fisher himself had the faults of drunkenness and licentiousness, and was guilty of embezzlement of trust funds. On coming home one night in a state of inebriety, he fell into a ditch, and died from eXposure.

O Thou, who in the heavens dost dwell
Whom, as it pleases, at thy will
Sends one to heaven and ten to hell,
  All for thy glory,
And not for any good or ill
  They 've done before thee.

I bless and praise thy matchless might,
When thousands thou hast left in night,
That I am here before thy sight
  For gifts and grace;
A burning and a shining light
  To all this place.

What was I, or my generation,
That I should get such exaltation?
I, who deserve such just damnation
  For broken laws,
Five thousand years 'fore my creation,
  Through Adam's cause.

When from my mother's womb I fell,
Thou might have plunged me into hell
To gnash my gums and weep and wail
  In burning lake,
Where damnèd devils roar and yell,
  Chained to a stake.

Yet I am here, a chosen sample,
To show thy grace is great and ample;
I 'm here a pillar in thy temple,
  Strong as a rock;
A guide, a buckler, and example
  To all thy flock.

O Lord, thou know'st what zeal I bear
When drinkers drink and swearers swear,

And singing here and dancing there
    With great and small,
For thou dost keep me by thy fear,
    Free from them all.

But yet, O Lord! confess I must
To random flings of fleshly lust,
And sometimes, too, with worldly trust
    Vile self gets in;
But thou rememb'rest we are dust
    Defiled in sin.

Thou know'st, O Lord, last night with Meg —
Thy pardon I sincerely beg;
May it ne'er be a living plague
    To my dishonor,
And I will make a solemn league
    Henceforth to shun her.

Besides, I further must allow,
With Lizzie's lass I got in tow;
That Friday, Lord, I must avow,
    When I came near her
I had been drinking, else, thou know,
    I ne'er would steer her.

Perhaps thou lets this fleshly thorn
Beset thy servant night and morn,
Lest he o'er high and proud should turn,
    'Cause he's so gifted;
If so thy hand must e'en be borne
    Until thou lift it.

Lord, bless thy chosen in this place,
For here thou hast a chosen race;
But God confound their stubborn face,
    And blast their name,
Who bring thy elders to disgrace
    And public shame.

Lord, mind Gawn Hamilton's deserts,
He drinks and swears and plays at cartes,
Yet has so many taking arts
    With great and small,
From God's own priests, the people's hearts,
    He steals them all.

And when we chastened him therefor,
Thou know'st he made us sick and sore,
And set the world in a roar
        Of laughing at us;
Curse thou his basket and his store,
        Kale and potatoes.

Lord, hear my earnest cry and prayer
Against the Presbyt'ry of Ayr;
Thy strong, right hand, Lord, make it bare
        Upon their heads;
Lord, weigh it down and do not spare
        For their misdeeds.

O Lord, my God, that glib-tongued Aiken,
My very heart and soul are quaking,
To think how we stood groaning, shaking,
        And sweat with dread,
While he with haughty lip and snaking,
        Held up his head.

Lord, in the day of vengeance try him,
Lord, visit them who did employ him,
And pass not in thy mercy by them,
        Nor hear their prayer,
But for thy people's sake destroy them,
        And do not spare.

But, Lord, remember me and mine
With mercies temporal and divine,
That I for wealth and grace may shine,
        Excelled by none;
And all the glory shall be thine,—
        Amen, amen.

———

EPITAPH ON HOLY WILLIE.

Here, holy Willie's sore-worn clay
    Takes up its last abode;
His soul has gone some other way,
    I fear, the left-hand road.

Stop, there he is, as sure's a gun,
    Poor, silly body, see him!
No wonder he is black and dun;
    Observe who's standing by him!

Your brimstone devilship, I see,
  Has got him there before ye,
But hold your cat-o'-nine-tails, pray,
  Till once you've heard my story.

Your pity I will not implore,
  Of pity you are lacking;
Justice, alas! has given him o'er,
  And mercy him forsaken.

But hear me, sir! bad as you are,
  Look somewhat to your credit;
To whip such fools would stain your name,
  If it were known you did it.

EPISTLE TO DAVIE,

A BROTHER POET.

While winds from off Ben–Lomond blow,
And bar the doors with drifting snow,
  And drive us to the fire;
I sit me down to pass the time,
And spin a verse or two of rhyme
  As fancy may inspire.
While frosty winds, the snowy drift
  Blow in the chimney cheek,
I sometimes grudge the great folks' gift,
  Yet barter do not seek:
    I pant less, and want less
      Their cheerless, big fireside
    But hanker and canker,
      To see their cursèd pride.

I find 't is hardly in one's power
To keep, at times, from being sour,
  To see how things are shared,
How best of folks are scant of diet,
While fools on countless thousands riot
  Nor care how others fared.
But, Davie, trouble not your head,
  Though we have little wealth,
We're fit to earn our daily bread
  As long as we have health;
    And care not, nor fear not,
      Old age ne'er mind a fig,
    The worst then, at last then,
      Is only but to beg.

To lie in kilns and barns at e'en,
When bones are crazed and blood is thin,
  Is doubtless great distress;
Yet then content could make us blest,
Ev'n then sometimes we'd snatch a taste
  Of truest happiness.
The honest heart that's free from all
  Intended fraud or guile,
However Fortune kick the ball,
  Has still some cause to smile:
    And mind still, you'll find still,
     A comfort this, though small,
    No more then, we'll care then,
     No further can we fall.

What though like commoners of air
We wander out, we know not where,
  With neither house nor hall;
Yet Nature's charms — the hills and woods,
The sweeping vales and foaming floods
  Are free alike to all.
In days when daisies deck the ground
  And blackbirds whistle clear,
With honest joy our hearts will bound
  To see the coming year:
    'Neath trees, when we please, then,
     We'll sit and hum a tune;
    In rhyme, then, and time, then
     We'll sing till day is done.

It's not in titles nor in rank,
It's not in wealth, like London bank
  To purchase peace and rest:
'Tis not to riches adding more,
'Tis not in books, nor yet in lore,
  To make us truly blest.
If happiness has not her seat
  And centre in the breast,
We may be wise or rich or great,
  And yet with gloom oppressed.
    No treasures, nor pleasures
     Could make us happy long;
    The heart's still the part still
     That makes us right or wrong.

Think you that such as you and I,
Who drudge and drive through wet and dry
  With never-ceasing toil:
Think you are we less blest than they

Who scarce observe us on their way
  As hardly worth their while?
Alas! how oft in haughty mood
  God's creatures they oppress,
Or else neglecting all that's good
  They riot in excess!
    Both careless and fearless
      Of either heaven or hell·
    Esteeming and deeming
      It all an idle tale!

Then let us cheerful acquiesce,
Nor make our scanty pleasures less
  By pining at our state;
And, even should misfortunes come,
Though I myself have met with some,
  I'm thankful for them yet;
They give the wit of age to youth,
  And wisdom's ways instil —
They make us see the naked truth,
  The real good and ill:
    Though losses and crosses
      Be lessons right severe,
    There's wit there, you'll get there
      You'll find no other where.

But mind me, Davie, ace of hearts!
(To call you less would wrong the cartes,
  And flattery I detest),
This life has joys for you and I,
Joys that the wealthy scarce can buy, —
  Yea, joys the very best.
There's all the pleasures of the heart,
  Where love and friendship's seen;
You have your Meg, your dearest part,
  And I, my darling Jean!
    It warms me, it charms me,
      To mention but her name;
    It cheers me, endears me,
      And sets me all on flame.

Oh, all ye Powers who rule above!
O Thou, whose very self art love!
  Thou know'st my words sincere!
The life-blood streaming through my heart,
Or my more dear, immortal part,
  Is not more fondly dear!
When heart-corroding care and grief
  Deprive my soul of rest,

Her dear idea brings relief
And solace to my breast.
Thou Being, all-seeing,
Oh, hear my fervent prayer!
Still take her, and make her
Thy most peculiar care.

All hail, ye tender feelings dear!
The smile of love, the friendly tear,
The sympathetic glow!
Long since this rude world's thorny ways
Had numbered out my weary days,
Had it not been for you!
Fate still has blest me with a friend
In every care and ill;
And oft a more endearing band,
A tie more tender still.
It lightens, it brightens
The tenebrific scene,
To meet with and greet with
My Davie or my Jean.

Oh, how that name inspires my style!
The words come skipping, rank and file
In all their happy train;
The ready measure runs as fine
As if the famous Muses nine
Were hovering o'er my pen.
My spavined Pegasus will limp
Till once he's fairly hot,
Then wings aspread, and limbs so jimp,
He'll fleetly run or trot,
But lest then, the beast then,
Should rue this hasty ride—
I'll light now, this night now,
And groom his sweaty hide.

ADDRESS TO THE TOOTHACHE.

WRITTEN WHEN THE AUTHOR WAS GRIEVOUSLY TOR-
MENTED BY THAT DISORDER.

My curse upon the venom'd thing
That my poor gums are torturing;
And through my head gives many a sting
With gnawing vengeance;
Tearing my nerves with throbbing ring
Like racking engines.

When fevers burn, or ague freezes,
Rheumatics gnaw, or cholic squeezes,
Our neighbors' sympathy may ease us
      With pitying moan;
But thou — thou hell of all diseases
      Still mocks our groan.

Adown my beard fast runs the spittle,
I kick the stools and pots and kettle,
While round me laugh the children little,
      I wish, "'od rot 'em,"
A thistle or a stinging nettle
      Were in their bottom.

Of all the numerous human ills,
Poor crops, bad bargains, stubborn wills,
The tricks of knaves, and tradesmen's bills,
      That make us swear;
Thou, Toothache! who but seldom kills
      Art worst to bear.

Where'er that place be priests' call hell,
Whence all the tones of misery yell,
And labelled plagues, their numbers tell
      In dreadful row,
Thy figures sure must all excel
      Of human woe.

O thou grim, mischief-making De'il,
That makes the notes of discord squeal
Till men in madness tramp and reel
      In gore a shoe thick;
Give all the foes of Scotland's weal
      A twelve-months' toothache.

EPISTLE TO THE REV. JOHN McMATH.

SEPTEMBER 17, 1785.

While round the stook the reapers cower
To shun the bitter, blinding shower,
Or song and chorus rant and roar
      To pass the time,
To you I dedicate the hour
      In idle rhyme.

My Muse, tired out with many a sonnet
On gown and band and holy bonnet,
Has grown right scared now she has done it,
          Lest they should blame her
And rouse their holy thunder on it
          And anathem her.

I own 't was rash and rather hardy
That I, a simple country bardie,
Should meddle with a pack so sturdy
          Who, if they'd known me,
Could, in a sermon long and wordy
          Loose hell upon me.

But I got mad at their grimaces,
Their sighing, canting, grace-proud faces,
Their three-mile prayers, and half-mile graces,
          Their rubber conscience,
Whose greed, revenge, and pride disgraces
          Worse than their nonsense.

There's Gawn, defamed worse than a beast,
Who has more honor in his breast
Than many scores as good's the priest
          Who so abused him;
And may a bard not have his jest,
          The way they've used him.

See him, the poor man's friend in need,
The gentleman in word and deed,
And shall his fame and honor bleed
          By barking poodles;
And not a muse erect her head
          To shame the noodles.

O Pope, had I thy satires' darts
To give the rascals their deserts,
I'd rip their rotten, hollow hearts,
          And tell aloud
Their juggling hocus-pocus arts
          To cheat the crowd.

God knows I'm not the thing I should be,
Nor even am the thing I could be,
But twenty times I rather would be
          An atheist clean,
Than under gospel colors hid be
          Just for a screen.

An honest man may like a glass,
An honest man may like a lass,
But to revenge and malice base
      He'll ne'er bow down,
And then cry zeal for gospel laws,
      Like some we've known.

Their bulls they issue like the pope,
They talk of love and faith and hope,
For what? to give their malice scope
      On some poor wight;
Against them all he cannot cope,
      He's ruined quite.

All hail, Religion! maid divine!
Pardon a muse so mean as mine,
Who in her rough, imperfect line
      Thus dares to name thee;
To stigmatise false friends of thine,
      Can ne'er defame thee.

Though blotched and foul with many a stain,
And far unworthy of thy train,
With trembling voice I tune my strain
      To join with those
Who boldly dare thy cause maintain
      In spite of foes.

In spite of crowds, in spite of mobs
In spite of undermining jobs,
In spite of dark banditti stabs
      At worth and merit,
By scoundrels vile in holy robes,
      But hellish spirit.

O Ayr, my dear, my native ground,
Within thy Presbyterial bound,
A liberal, candid band is found
      Of public teachers;
As men, as Christians, too, renowned,
      And manly preachers.

Sir, in that circle you are named;
Sir, in that circle you are famed;
And some, by whom your doctrine's blamed
      (Which gives you honor),
Even, sir, by them your heart's esteemed,
      And winning manner.

Pardon this freedom I am taking,
And if intrusion I 've been making,
Impute it not to kindness lacking,
       When this I send you,
But who, when all the world forsaking,
       Would still befriend you.

———

EPISTLE TO WILLIAM SIMPSON

OF OCHILTREE.

MAY, 1785.

I got your rhyming letter, Willie;
With gratitude I thank you really,
Though I must say I would be silly
       And weakly vain
Should I believe your praise so wily
       And flattering strain.

But still, I think you kindly meant it·
I should be loth to think you hinted
Ironic satire, sidling slanted
       On my poor Musie;
Though in the flattering terms you sent it
       I scarce excuse you.

I should be crazy more than double
Could I but dare a hope to trouble
To vie with Ramsay, with my scribble,
       On rolls of fame;
Or Fergusson, the poet noble,
       Of deathless name.

O Fergusson, thy glorious parts
Ill suited law's dry musty arts!
My curse upon your whinstone hearts
       Ye Edinboro' gentry!
The tenth of what you waste on cartes
       Would filled his pantry,

Yet, when a tale comes in my head,
Or love my heart has all mislead,
(And many a time I 'm almost dead
       From that disease),
I up and tune my rustic reed;
       It gives me ease.

Old Coila now mature has grown;
She's gotten poets of her own,—
Bards who her virtues will make known
      In tuneful lays,
Till echoes all resound the tone
      Of well-sung praise.

No poet thought it worth his while
To set her name in measured style;
She lay like some benighted isle
      Beyond New Holland,
Off where wild southern oceans boil,
      And almost no land.

Ramsay and Fergusson have won
From Forth and Tay their benison;
Yarrow and Tweed to many a tune
      O'er Scotland rings,
While Irvine, Lugar, Ayr, and Doon,
      Nobody sings.

The Rhine, the Tiber, Thames, and Seine,
Glide sweet in many a tuneful line;
But, Willie, set your foot to mine
      And lift your crest —
We'll make our streams and brooks to shine
      Up with the best.

We'll sing Old Coila's plains and fells,
Her moors, red-brown with heather bells,
Her banks and braes, her dens and dells,
      Where Wallace glorious
Wielded the sword, and story tells,
      Came off victorious!

At Wallace' name what Scottish blood
But boils up in a spring-tide flood!
Oft have our fearless fathers stood
      By Wallace' side,
And still to vict'ry red-wet strode,
      Or glorious died.

Oh, sweet are Coila's fields and woods,
When lintwhites chant among the buds,
And jinking hares, in amorous moods,
      Their love enjoy,
While cushats fly to shield their broods
      With wailful cry.

Even winter bleak has charms for me,
When winds rave over wood and lea,
Or frosts on hills of Ochiltree
          Are hoary gray;
Or blinding drifts, with madd'ning glee,
          Darken the day.

O Nature! all thy calms and storms,
To feeling, pensive hearts have charms,
Whither the summer kindly warms
          To life and light,
Or winter howls in wild alarms,
          The long, dark night.

The Muse, no poet ever found her,
Till by himself he learned to wander,
Adown some wimpling brook's meander
          Nor think it long:
'T is sweet to stray, and pensive ponder
          A heart-felt song.

The worldly race may drudge and drive,
Like senseless swine, may stretch and strive;
To me fair Nature's all alive
          With sweetest pleasure.
We'll let the busy, grubbing hive
          Hum o'er their treasure.

Farewell, my rhyme-composing brother!
We've been too long unknown to other;
Now let us lay our heads together
          In love fraternal.
May Envy go to regions nether,
          Black fiend infernal!

While Highlandmen hate tolls and taxes,
While "Mother Earth" still older waxes,
And while she safely on her axis
          Diurnal turns,
Count on a friend, in faith and practice,
          In ROBERT BURNS.

POSTSCRIPT.

My memory's not worth a pin,
I had almost forgotten clean,
You bade me write you what they mean
          By this New Light,
'Bout which our herds so oft have been
          Most like to fight.

In days when mankind were but boys
And college learning did despise,
They took no pains their speech to poise,
      But spoke out free
In good, old-fashioned, honest ways,
      Like you and me.

In those old times, they thought the moon
Just like a shirt, or pair of shoon,
Wore by degrees, until when done
      Went past their viewing,
And by and by, and that right soon,
      They got a new one.

This passed for certain — undisputed,
It ne'er came in their head to doubt it,
Till some got up and would confute it
      And called it wrong;
And wrangling noise they made about it,
      Both loud and long.

Some herds, well learned upon the book
Held that old folks the thing mistook
'T was just the old moon turned a nook
      And out of sight;
Then backward came, and seemed to look
      Again more bright.

This was denied then re-affirmed,
The herd and flock were sore alarmed,
The reverend graybeards raved and stormed
      That beardless lads
Should think they better were informed
      Than their old dads.

From less to more it came to sticks,
From words and oaths to blows and licks,
And many a one got cuffs and kicks
      And heels upturned,
While some to learn them for their tricks.
      Were hanged and burned.

The game was played in many lands,
But Old Lights bore such heavy hands
That, faith! the young took to the sands
      With nimble shanks,
Till squires forbade, by strict commands,
      Such bloody pranks.

The New Lights crept into their hole·
All thought them ruined, head to sole;
Till now almost on every knoll
           You 'll find one placed,
And some their New Light fair extol
           Just quite barefaced.

No doubt the Old Light flocks are bleating,
Their zealous heads are vexed and sweating.
Myself, I've seen them cry with fretting
           And angry spite,
To hear the moon betrayed by cheating,
           In word and write.

But shortly they will scare the loons!
Some Old Light herds in neighbor towns
Intend in things they call balloons
           To take a flight,
And stay a month among the moons,
           And see them right.

Good observation they will give them,
And when the old moon's going to leave them,
The last bit shreds, they'll quickly shove them
           Just in their pouch,
And when the New Light herds perceive them,
           I think they 'll crouch,

So you've observed that all this clatter,
Is nothing but a " moonshine matter;"
But though dull prose-folk Latin sputter
           In logic bawl,
I hope we bards know something better,
           Than mind such brawl.

———

SECOND EPISTLE TO DAVIE,

A BROTHER POET.

I'm more than six times now your debtor
For your old-fashioned friendly letter.
Though I must say, I doubt you flatter
           In what you've writ me;
For my poor, silly, rhyming clatter,
           Some less would suit me.

Whole be your heart, your head also·
Long may you ply your fiddle-bow,
To lighten up your weary brow
    From worldly cares,
Till children's children pat your pow
    And old gray hairs.

But, Davie lad, you must be checked,
I'm told the Muse you do neglect;
And if it's so, you should be licked
    Until you wince;
A man like you should ne'er elect
    To be a dunce.

For me, I'm on Parnassus' brink,
Twisting the words to make them clink;
At times confused by love and drink
    With jades or masons;
And sometimes, but too late I think,
    Fine sober lessons.

Of all the thoughtless sons of man,
Commend me to the poet clan;
Except it be some idle plan
    Of rhyming clink,
No bit that I can understand
    They ever think.

No thought, no view, no scheme of living,
No cares to give us joy or grieving;
Our purses still the hand receiving;
    And while aught's there,
Then on life's road contented driving,
    And free from care.

Hail, glorious rhyme! Ah, what a treasure!
My chief, almost my only pleasure;
At home, at field, at work, or leisure,
    The Muse, poor hussy,
Though rough and ragged in her measure,
    She's seldom lazy.

Hold to the Muse, my dainty Davie;
The world may hold you still it's slavey,
But for the Muse, she'll never leave you
    Though e'er so poor,
And begging round, with sorrow heavy,
    From door to door.

THE HOLY FAIR.

Upon a summer Sunday morn,
  When Nature's face is fair,
I walked abroad to view the corn
  And breathe the morning air.
The rising sun o'er Galston moors
  With glorious light was glancing·
The hares leaped through the field and furze,
  The lark's song was entrancing
      And sweet that day.

As lightsomely I gazed around
  Upon a scene so cheering,
Three lasses, early on the ground,
  Came up my way a-steering;
Two had on mantles, doleful black,
  Of which, one had gray lining;
The third, that held herself aback,
  Was in the fashion shining
      So gay that day.

The first two were like sisters twin,
  In feature, form, and clothing;
With visage withered, long, and thin,
  Which filled my heart with loathing.
The third came up, hop-step and leap,
  And just as soon's she saw me,
She made a curtsy low and deep;
  Her smile was sweet and balmy
      And kind that day.

I doffed my cap and said, "Sweet lass,
  You really seem to know me;
I know your face, your name I'll guess,
  If you will but allow me."
She took me warmly by the hands,
  Her words with mirth were spoken;
Quoth she, "Some of the ten commands
  For my sake you have broken,
      Some former day.

"My name is Fun—your crony dear,
  I hate all aristocracy,
And this is Superstition, here,
  The other is Hypocrisy.
I'm going to Mauchline holy fair,
  To have some sport and chaffing;

If you'll go there, at yonder pair
  We will get famous laughing
    And sport this day."

"Agreed,", I said, "when I have got
  My Sunday clothes for sparking,
I'll meet you on the holy spot,—
  We'll have some fine remarking."
Then home I went with cheerful stride,
  And soon I made me ready;
The roads were clad from side to side
  With many a weary body,
    In droves that day.

Here, farmers fine, in riding gear,
  Went jogging by their cotters;
There, youthful chaps, in broadcloth dear,
  Are springing o'er the gutters.
The lasses, tripping, barefoot throng,
  In silks and scarlet glitter,
With sweet-milk cheese to whet the tongue,
  And oatmeal cakes and butter,
    So nice that day.

Then at the contribution box,
  Well heaped with not a few pence,
The Deacon eyes me like a fox,—
  I have to put in twopence.
Then in we go amid the throng,
  On every side they're coming,
Some carrying chairs and stools along,
  While others' talk is humming
    Around, that day.

Here stands a shed to fend the showers
  And screen our country gentry,
There Racer Jess and two-three w——s
  Are blinking at the entry.
Here sits a row of tattling jades,
  With heaving breast and bare neck,
And there a pack of weaver lads
  Blackguarding from Kilmarnock
    For fun this day.

Then some are thinking of their sins,
  And some their clothes are eyeing;
One damns the feet that soiled his shins,
  Another's praying, sighing.

A sample, here, of the elect,
  With screwed-up grace-proud faces;
O'er there, a set of chaps are packed,
  Sly winking at the lasses
          In chairs that day.

Oh, happy is that man and blest!
  No wonder that it pride him!
When one dear lass that he likes best
  Comes clinking down beside him!
With arm reposed on her chairback,
  He sweetly does compose him,
Which, by degrees, slips round her neck
  And hand upon her bosom,
          So sly that day.

Now all the congregation are
  In silent expectation;
For Moodie climbs the holy stair
  With tidings of damnation.
Should Satan, as in ancient days,
  'Mong sons of God present him,
The very sight of Moodie's face
  Would banish and prevent him
          With fright that day.

Hear how he clears the points of faith,
  With rattling and with thumping!
Now meekly calm, now wild in wrath,
  He's stamping and he's jumping!
His lengthened chin, his turned-up snout
  His weirdly squeal and gestures,
Oh, how they fire the heart devout,
  Like cantharidian plasters,
          On such a day.

But hark! the tent has changed its voice
  There's peace and rest no longer·
For all the real judges rise,
  They cannot sit for anger.
Smith opens out his cold harangues
  On practice and on morals,
And off the godly pour in throngs,
  To give the jugs and barrels
          A lift that day.

What signifies his barren shine
  Of moral powers and reason?
His English style and gesture fine
  Are all clean out of season.
Like Socrates or Antonine
  Or some old pagan heathen,
The moral man he does define
  But ne'er a word of faith in,
        That's right that day.

In good time comes an antidote
  Against such poisoned nostrum,
For Peebles, from the Waterfoot,
  Ascends the holy rostrum;
See, up he's got the Word of God,
  And meek and prim has viewed it,
Then Common Sense takes to the road,
  And off and up the Cowgate
        With haste that day.

Wee Miller next the guard relieves
  And orthodoxy gabbles,
Though in his heart he well believes
  And thinks it old wives' fables:
But faith! the prig, he wants a manse,
  So cautiously he hums them,
Although his carnal wit and sense
  About half-way o'ercomes them,
        At times that day.

The ale-house now is filling up
  With pot-house commentators,
Some crying out for cakes and cup,
  And some the pint-dish clatters;
While thick and throng, and loud and long,
  With logic and with Scripture,
They raise a din that, in the end,
  Is like to breed a rupture
        Of wrath that day.

Inspiring drink! it gives us more
  Than either school or college;
It wakens wit and kindles lore
  And crams us full of knowledge.
If whiskey gill or penny ale
  Or any stronger potion,
On drinking deep, it will not fail
  To tickle up our notion
        By night or day.

The lads and lasses, gladly bent,
  To mind both soul and body,
Sit round the table, well content,
  And steer about the toddy.
On this one's dress, and that one's look,
  They're making observations,
While some are cosey in the nook,
  And forming assignations
        To meet some day.

But now the Lord's own trumpet toots
  Till all the hills are roaring,
And echoes back return the shouts,
  Black Russell is outpouring;
His piercing words, like Highland swords,
  Divide the joints and marrows;
His talk of hell where devils dwell;
  Our very soul it harrows
        With fright that day.

A vast, unbottomed, boundless pit
  Filled full of flaming brimstone,
Where water on the scorching heat
  Acts as it would on limestone!
The half-asleep start up with fear
  And think they hear it roaring,
When presently it does appear,
  'Twas but some neighbor snoring,
        Asleep that day.

'Twould take too long to tell the tale
  Of all this famous session,
And how they crowded to the ale
  Just after the dismission;
How drink went round in jugs and cups
  Among the forms and benches;
And cheese and bread from women's laps
  Was dealt about in lunches
        And lumps that day.

In comes a matronly goodwife
  And sits down by the fire,
She draws her cheese and eke her knife;
  The lasses they are shyer.
The old goodman about the grace,
  From side to side they bother,
But soon begins with serious face,
  And makes it long's as a tether
        Of cow that day.

Alas for him that gets no lass,
  Or lasses that have nothing!
Small need has he to say a grace,
  Or soil his Sunday clothing.
O wives, you know, when you were young
  How bonny lads you wanted;
The lasses' heads with shame will hang
  If bread and cheese be scanted
          On such a day.

Now Clinkumbell, with rattling tow,
  Cries out his usual tune;
Some swagger home the best they know,
  Some wait till afternoon.
At dykes the fellows halt a blink,
  Till lasses strip their shoon;
With faith and hope, and love and drink,
  They're all in famous tune
          For talk that day.

How many hearts this day converts
  Of sinners and of lasses!
Their hearts of stone, ere night, are gone
  As soft as any flesh is.
There's some are full of love divine,
  And some of brandy fuddle;
And many jobs, that day begun,
  May end in kiss and cuddle
          Some other day.

EPISTLE TO JOHN LAPRAIK.

APRIL 1, 1785.

While briars and woodbines budding green,
And partridge screaming loud at e'en,
And leaping hare, with pleasure keen
          Inspires my Muse,
These lines from one you've never seen
          You'll pray excuse.

On Fast-day night we had a rocking,
To sit and chat and weave our stocking·
And there was lots of fun and joking,
          You need not doubt;
At length we had a hearty yoking
          At song about.

There was one song among the rest,
(Above them all it pleased me best),
That some kind husband had addressed
          To some sweet wife;
It thrilled the heartstrings in my breast,
          Keen to the life.

The words so grandly did reveal
What gen'rous, manly bosoms feel;
Thinks I, "Can this be Pope, or Steele,
          Or Beattie's work?"
They told me 'twas a poet leal,
          In old Muirkirk.

My curiosity inspired,
About him further I enquired;
Then all that knew him round declared,
          He had some brains,
And rhyming gift with genius fired,
          Ran through his veins.

That, set him to a pint of ale,
And whether wise or merry tale
Or rhyming songs, he'd never fail,
          Or witty catches;
'Tween Inverness and Teviotdale,
          He had few matches.

Then up I got and swore (no harm in't),
Though I should pawn my nether garment,
Or die like cat or other varmint
          At some dyke-back,
I'd buy a gill of reeking ferment
          To hear you talk.

But, first and foremost, I shall tell,
Almost as soon as I could spell
I to the versifying fell,
          Though rude and rough:
To please myself, and friends as well,
          It's good enough.

I am no poet in a sense,
But just a rhymer, like by chance
And have to learning no pretence
          But 'tis no matter!
Whene'er my Muse does on me glance,
          I jingle at her.

Your critic folk may cock their nose,
And say, "How can you e'er propose,
You, who know hardly verse from prose,
  To make a song?"
But, by your leave, my learned foes,
  You may be wrong.

What's all your jargon of your schools,
Your Latin names for horns and stools;
If honest Nature made you fools,
  Throw by your grammars
And take to spades and farming tools,
  Or swinging hammers.

Dull blockheads, whose vain hope in cash is,
Confuse their brains in college classes;
They go in colts, and come out asses,
  Plain truth to speak;
And think to climb up steep Parnassus
  By dint of Greek.

Give me one spark of Nature's fire,
That's all the learning I desire;
Then, though I drudge through dub and mire
  At plough or cart,
My Muse, though homely in attire,
  May touch the heart.

Oh, for a spark of Ramsay's glee,
Or Fergusson, the bold and free,
Or bright Lapraik's, my friend to be,
  If I can hit it!
That would be good enough for me,
  If I could get it.

No doubt you've friends both old and new,
Though real friends I think are few·
Yet, if you want a friend that's true,
  I'm on your list,
Still, if you think you'd maybe rue,
  I wont insist.

My self-esteem does not excel,
Nor do I like my faults to tell;
But friends and folks that wish me well,
  They sometimes praise me;
Though I must own as many still
  As far debase me,

There's one bit fault for which they blame me;
I like the lasses — Heaven tame me!
For many a penny's wheedled from me
   At dance or fair;
I might say more that ought to shame me,
   But I'll forbear.

But Mauchline race, or Mauchline fair,
I shall be proud to meet you there;
We'll give one night's discharge to Care,
   If we foregather,
And have a swap of rhyming ware
   With one another.

We'll make the whiskey bottle clatter,
And christen him with boiling water,
And sit us down and make it scatter
   To cheer our heart;
And, faith! we'll be acquainted better
   Before we part.

Away, you selfish, worldly race,
Who think decorum, sense, and grace,
Ev'n love and friendship should give place
   To catch the coin!
I do not like to see your face,
   Nor bear your frown.

But you whom social pleasure charms,
Whose hearts the tide of kindness warms,
Who hold your being on the terms,
   "Each aid the others,"
Come to my bowl, come to my arms,
   My friends, my brothers!

But now I see I'll have to hustle,
My old goose-quill's worn to the gristle;
Two lines from you will make me whistle
   Both gay and fervent;
I now subscribe my first epistle,
   Your friend and servant.

SECOND EPISTLE TO JOHN LAPRAIK.

APRIL 21, 1785.

While cattle at the barn are lowing,
And ploughing horses homeward going,
This hour I take, at evening's glowing,
  To own I'm debtor
To you, my friend, by your allowing
  For your kind letter.

Fatigued and sore, with weary legs,
Rattling the corn out o'er the rigs,
Or dealing through among the nags
  Their ten-hour's bite,
My awkward Muse sore pleads and begs
  I would not write.

The lame, unkempt, unwilling hussy,
She's soft at best, and somewhat lazy,
Quoth she, "You know we've been so busy
  This month and more,
That, troth, my head is grown right dizzy
  And somewhat sore."

Her weak excuses made me mad;
"Conscience!" says I, "you thriftless jade.
I'll write, and that a hearty wad
  This very night,
So mind you don't affront your trade,
  But rhyme it right.

"Shall bold Lapraik, the king of hearts,
(If mankind were a pack of cartes),
Praise you so well for your deserts,
  In terms so friendly,
Yet you'll neglect to show your parts
  And thank him kindly?"

I got some paper in a blink,
And down went stumpie in the ink;
Said I, "Before I sleep a wink,
  I vow I'll close it,
And if the rhyme you will not clink
  By Jove, I'll prose it!"

So I've begun to scrawl, but whether
In rhyme or prose or both together,
Or some hodge-podge that's rightly neither
          I'll let it stand,
And scribble down something or other,
          Just clean off-hand.

My worthy friend, ne'er grudge and carp,
Though Fortune use you hard and sharp;
Come tune your merry moorland harp,
          With gleesome touch,
Ne'er mind how Fortune waft and warp,
          She's but a bitch.

She's giv'n me many a jerk and dig
Since I could straddle o'er a rig;
But, by the Lord! though I should beg,
          With old gray head,
I'll laugh and sing and shake my leg
          Till I am dead.

This makes the six and twentieth spring
I've seen the swallow on the wing;
Though Fortune's given me many a fling
          From year to year,
Yet still, despite her random sting,
          I, Rob, am here.

Do you envy the city gent,
Whose time on money bags is spent,
Or purse-proud big with cent. per cent.
          And portly paunch?
Although on civic honors bent,
          His name's a stench.

Or eke the haughty feudal thane,
With ruffled shirt and glancing cane,
Who thinks himself no sheep-shank bone,
          But lordly stalks,
While hats are waved with might and main
          As by he walks.

O Thou who giv'st us each good gift,
Give me of sense and wit a lift,
Then turn me, if Thou please, adrift
          O'er Scotland wide,
With cits or lords I would not shift,
          In all their pride!

Were this the charter of our state,
"On pain of hell be rich and great,"
Damnation then would be our fate
      Beyond remead;
But Heav'n be thanked, within that gate
      Lies not our creed.

For thus the royal mandate ran
When first the human race began,
The social, friendly, honest man
      Whate'er he be,
'T is he fulfils great Nature's plan —
      And none but he.

O mandate, glorious and divine!
The ragged followers of the Nine,
Poor, thoughtless devils! yet may shine
      In glorious light,
While sordid sons of Mammon's line
      Are dark as night.

Though here they scrape and squeeze and growl,
Their worthless handful of a soul
May in some future carcass howl,
      The forest's fright;
Or in some day-detesting owl
      May shun the light.

Then may Lapraik and Burns arise
To reach their native kindred skies,
And sing their pleasures, hopes, and joys
      In some mild sphere,
Still closer knit in friendship's ties
      Each passing year.

———

THIRD EPISTLE TO JOHN LAPRAIK.

SEPTEMBER 13, 1785.

Goodspeed I wish you, brother Johnny,
Good health, whole hands, and weather bonny;
When off the loaf in slices many
      You cut the bread,
May you ne'er want a brandy pony
      To clear your head.

May Boreas never spoil your corn,
Nor strew the sheaves all wrecked and torn,
Sending the stuff o'er fields forlorn
          Like driven wreck,
But may the utmost grain be borne
          Within the sack.

I'm busy too, and driving at it,
But bitter, windy showers have wet it,
So my old stumpie pen I got it
          To do its work;
But first took out my pen and whet it
          Like any clerk.

It's now two months that I'm your debtor
For your fine, nameless, dateless letter
Abusing me for harsh ill nature
          On holy men;
While not a hair yourself you're better,
          But more profane.

But let the kirk-folk ring their bells!
We'll call no jades from heathen hills
Nor drink the draughts from Grecian wells,
          That wit infuses;
But ale-house wives and whiskey stills
          Will be our muses.

Your friendship, sir, I will not quit it;
And if the favor you'll permit it,
Your hand in mine some day will knit it
          And witness take;
And when with social glass we've wet it,
          It will not break.

But if the beast and bridle's spared
Till calves are fit to join the herd,
And all the hay about the yard
          Is thatched and tight,
Your fireside will by me be shared
          Some winter night.

Then muse-inspiring aqua vitæ
Will make us both so brisk and witty,
That you'll forget you're old and gouty,
          And be as happy
As you were nine years less than thirty
          A gay young chappie.

But stooks are turned o'er with the blast;
The sun is sinking in the west,
So I must run among the rest
    And quit my chanter;
While I subscribe myself in haste,
    Yours, ROB, THE RANTER.

EPISTLE TO JAMES SMITH.

[A faithful friend of Burns and present with him at the Jolly Beggars'
carousal in " Poosie Nancy's."]

Dear Smith, I 'll write, if you 'd as lief,
My estimate of you in brief;
I think of warlocks you 're the chief,
    O'er human hearts,
And stoics e'en might come to grief
    Through your sly arts.

For me, dear sir, I 've freely sworn
By stars at night and sun at morn,
That twenty pairs of shoes I 've worn
    In frequent stride,
To reach the cheerful, welcome bourne
    Of your fireside.

That old capricious dame called Nature,
To recompense defective stature,
Has turned you off, a human creature
    On her first plan;
And in her freaks, on every feature
    She 's wrote, " The Man."

Just now I 'm seized with fit of rhyme,
My noddle's brisk and working prime,
My fancy 's bobbing up sublime
    At hasty summon;
Have you a leisure moment's time,
    To hear what 's comin'?

Some blight their neighbor's name in scribble,
Some rhyme (vain thought) for needful boodle,
And some to catch bright fame's soap bubble
    And raise a din;
But that 's an aim I never trouble,
    I rhyme for fun.

The star that rules my luckless lot,
Has fated me the russet coat,
And damn'd my purse with scarce a jot;
          But has seen fit
To bless me with a random shot
          Of country wit.

At times a vain conceit does hint,
To try my fate in good, black print,
But still, the more I'm that way bent,
          Something cries "Rob.
Take care, you'll find when money's spent,
          You've botched the job."

There's other poets much your betters,
Far seen in Greek, deep men of letters,
Have thought they had insured their debtors,
          All future ages;
Now moths deform in shapeless tatters,
          Their unknown pages.

Then farewell hopes of laurel-boughs,
To garland my poetic brows!
Henceforth I'll rove where busy ploughs
          Are whistling throng,
And teach the oxen and the cows
          My rustic song.

I'll wander on with aimless heed,
How never halting moments speed,
Till Fate shall snap the brittle thread;
          Then, all unknown
I'll lay me with inglorious dead,
          Forgot and gone.

But why of death begin a tale?
Just now we're living sound and hale,
Then top and maintop crowd the sail,
          Heave Care o'er side!
And large, before Enjoyment's gale,
          Let's take the tide.

This life, so far's I understand,
Is all enchanted fairy land,
Where Pleasure is the magic wand,
          That, wielded right,
Makes hours like minutes, hand in hand,
          Dance by full light.

To wield this wand then let's engage,
For, when we've turned life's fiftieth page,
See weary, crazy, joyless Age,
    With wrinkled face,
Come limping, coughing, sad and sage,
    With creeping pace.

When once life's day draws near the gloaming,
Then farewell vacant, careless roaming,
And farewell cheerful tankards foaming,
    And social noise;
And farewell, dear deluding woman
    The joy of joys!

O Life! how pleasant is thy morning,
Young Fancy's rays the hills adorning!
Cold-pausing Caution's lesson scorning,
    We frisk away,
Like schoolboys, at the expected warning,
    To joy and play.

We wander there, we wander here,
We pluck the rose, without a fear,
Unmindful that the thorn is near
    Among the leaves;
And though the puny wound appear,
    Short time it grieves.

Some, lucky, find a flowery spot,
For which they never toiled or sweat,
They drink the sweet and eat the fat
    Nor care, nor pain;
And, haply, eye the lowly hut,
    With high disdain.

With steady aim, some fortune chase,
Keen hope does every sinew brace,
Through fair, through foul, they urge the race,
    And seize the prey;
Then quietly in some cosey place,
    They close the day.

And some, like me, whose life unnerving,
Live on, no rules or roads observing,
To right or left, eternal swerving,
    They zig-zag on;
Till cursed with age, obscure and starving,
    They sigh and groan.

Alas! what bitter toil and straining —
But truce with peevish, poor complaining!
Is Fortune's fickle Luna waning?
        We'll get along!
Beneath what light she has remaining,
        Let's sing our song.

My pen I here fling to the door,
And kneel, "Ye Powers!" I you implore,
"Though I should roam the world o'er,
        In all her climes,
Grant me but this, I ask no more,
        A wealth of rhymes.

"Give dripping roasts to gourmands lazy,
Until their beards shine fat and greasy:
Give handsome clothes to titled hussy
        And big dragoons,
And ale and whiskey, till they're dizzy,
        To tinker loons.

"A title, Dempster merits it,
A garter give to Willie Pitt;
Give wealth to some be-ledgered cit,
        In cent. per cent.;
But give me real sterling wit
        And I'm content.

"If you are pleased to keep me hale,
I'll sit down o'er my scanty meal
(If gruel thin or watery kale)
        With cheerful face,
As long's the Muses do not fail
        To say the grace."

My eye an anxious look ne'er throws
Behind my ear, or by my nose;
I dodge beneath Misfortune's blows
        As well's I may,
Sworn foe to Sorrow, Care, and Prose,
        I rhyme away.

O you wise folks who live by rule,
Grave, tideless-blooded, calm and cool
Compared with you — O fool! fool! fool!
        How much unlike!
Your hearts are just a standing pool,
        Your lives, a dyke.

No hair-brained, sentimental traces
In your unlettered, nameless faces!
In arioso trills and graces
    You never stray,
But gravissimo, solemn basses,
    You hum away.

You are so grave, no doubt you're wise;
No wonder though you do despise
The harum-scarum, reckless boys,
    The rattling squad,
I see you upward cast your eyes,
    You know the road.

Whilst I — but I will hold me there —
With you I'll scarce go anywhere —
I'll close my scrawl now, Jamie dear,
    And quit my song,
Content with you to make a pair,
    Among the throng.

TO A HAGGIS.

Fair fall your honest, jovial face,
Great chieftain of the pudding race!
Above them all you take your place,
    Or tripe or sausage.
Well are you worthy of a grace,
    Or rhyming message.

The groaning trencher there you fill
Your buttock like a distant hill,
Your skewer would help to mend a mill
    In time of need;
While through your pores the dews distil
    Like amber bead.

See rustic, nerved by appetite,
Cut up your bag with ready slight,
Trenching your gushing entrails bright
    Like any ditch;
And then, oh, what a glorious sight,
    Warm-reeking, rich!

Then horn for horn they stretch and strive,
Deil take the hindmost! on they drive
Just fain to quit when scarce alive
      And stomach warns;
Then old goodman, most like to rive
      The thanks returns.

Is there that o'er his French ragout,
Or stuff would make a sow look blue,
Or fricassee would make her spew
      In sheer disgust,
Looks down with sneering, scornful view,
      On such repast.

Poor devil! see him o'er his trash,
As pithless as a withered rush,
His spindle-shank a fine whip lash,
      His fist a nut:
Through bloody flood or field to dash,
      Oh, how unfit!

But mark the rustic, haggis-fed,
The trembling earth resounds his tread,
Clap in his mighty hand a blade
      He'll make it whistle,
And legs, and arms, and heads will shed,
      Like tops of thistle.

Ye Powers who make mankind your care,
And dish them out their bill of fare,
Old Scotland wants no foreign ware
      That scrimp and scrag is;
But if you want her grateful prayer,
      Give her a haggis.

VERSES WRITTEN UNDER VIOLENT GRIEF.

Accept the gift a friend sincere
  Would on thy worth be pressing;
Remembrance oft may start a tear,
But oh! that tenderness forbear,
  Though 'twould my sorrows lessen.

My morning rose so clear and fair,
  I thought rude storms would never
Bedew the scene; but grief and care
In wildest fury have made bare
  My peace, my hope, forever!

You think I'm glad; oh, I pay well
  For all the joy I borrow,
In solitude — then, then I feel
I cannot to myself conceal
  My deeply-rankling sorrow.

Farewell! within thy bosom free
  A sigh at times may waken;
A tear may dim thine eye's bright ray,
For Scotia's son — once like thee gay,
  Now hopeless, and forsaken.

A BARD'S EPITAPH.

[Wordsworth says, — " Here is a sincere and solemn avowal — a public declaration from his own will — a confession at once devout, poetical, and human — a history in the shape of a prophecy."]

Is there a whim-inspirèd fool,
Too fast for thought, too hot for rule,
Too shy to seek, too proud to pule?
    Let him draw near;
And o'er this grave, with bosom full,
    Let drop a tear.

Is there a bard of rustic song,
Who, noteless, steals the crowds among,
That weekly this area throng?
    Oh, pass not by!
But with a frater-feeling strong,
    Here heave a sigh.

Is there a man, whose judgment clear
Can others teach the course to steer,
Yet runs, himself, life's mad career,
    Wild as the wave?
Here pause — and, through the starting tear,
    Survey this grave.

The poor inhabitant below
Was quick to learn, and wise to know,
And keenly felt the friendly glow,
    And softer flame;
But thoughtless follies laid him low,
    And stain'd his name.

Reader, attend — whether thy soul
Soars fancy's flights beyond the pole,
Or darkling grubs this earthly hole,
          In low pursuit;
Know, prudent, cautious self-control
          Is wisdom's root.

EPISTLE TO A YOUNG FRIEND.

I long have thought, my youthful friend
    A something to have sent you,
Though it should serve no other end
    Than just a kind memento;
But how the theme may get along,
    Let time and chance determine,
Perhaps it may turn out a song,
    Perhaps turn out a sermon.

You'll try the world full soon, my lad,
    And, Andrew dear, believe me,
You'll find mankind a sorry squad,
    And greatly they may grieve you;
For care and trouble set your thought
    Even when your end you've reached it,
You'll find your views may come to naught,
    Though ev'ry nerve you've stretched it.

I'll not say men are villains all,
    The hardened wretch, convicted,
Who knows no check but legal thrall,
    Are to a few restricted;
But, oh! mankind are very weak,
    And little to be trusted,
If self the wavering balance shake,
    It's rarely right adjusted.

Yet they who fall in fortune's strife,
    Their fate we should not censure,
For still th' important end of life,
    They equally may answer;
A man may have an honest heart,
    Though fortune ill may fare him,
A man may take a neighbor's part,
    And have no cash to spare him.

Aye free off-hand your story tell,
    When with a bosom crony,

But somethings, it might be as well,
　To scarcely tell to any;
Conceal yourself as well's you can,
　From critical dissection,
But keenly look through other men
　With sharpened, sly inspection.

The sacred flame of well-placed love
　Luxuriantly indulge it,
But never tempt th' illicit rove,
　Though nothing should divulge it;
I waive the quantum of the sin,
　The hazard of concealing;
But, oh! it hardens all within,
　And petrifies the feeling.

To catch dame Fortune's golden smile,
　Assiduous wait upon her,
And gather wealth by every wile
　That's justified by honor;
Not for to hide it in a hedge.
　Nor for a train attendant,
But for the glorious privilege
　Of being independent.

The fear of hell's a hangman's whip
　To hold the wretch in order,
But where you feel your honor grip,
　Let that aye be your border;
Its slightest touches, instant pause —
　Debar all side pretences,
And resolutely keep its laws,
　Uncaring consequences.

The great Creator to revere,
　Must sure become the creature;
But still the preaching cant forbear
　And even the rigid feature;
Yet ne'er with wits profane to range,
　Be complaisance extended;
An atheist laugh's a poor exchange,
　For Deity offended.

When ranting round in Pleasure's ring,
　Religion may be blinded;
Or if she give a random sting,
　It may be little minded;

But when on life we're tempest-driven,
  A conscience but a canker —
A correspondence fixed with Heaven
  Is sure a noble anchor!

Adieu, dear, amiable youth!
  Your heart can ne'er be wanting!
May prudence, fortitude, and truth
  Erect your brow undaunting!
In ploughman phrase, "God send you speed,"
  Still daily to grow wiser:
And may you more the counsel heed,
  Than ever did the adviser.

HALLOWEEN.

Upon that night, when fairies light
  On Cassilis Downans dance;
Or o'er the lays, in splendid blaze,
  On sprightly coursers prance;
Or for Colean they guide the rein,
  Beneath the moon's pale beams;
There up the cove to stray and rove,
  Among the rocks and streams
      To sport that night.

Among the bonny winding banks
  Where Doon runs, wimpling clear,
Where Bruce once ruled the martial ranks,
  And shook his Carrick spear;
Some merry, friendly, country-folks,
  Together did convene,
To burn their nuts, and pull their stalks,
  And hold their Halloween,
      So gay that night.

The lasses trim, and cleanly neat,
  More winsome than when showy;
With faces radiant, kind, and sweet,
  True hearts, without alloy:
The lads so spruce, with ribbons fine,
  Well knotted on their garters,
Some shy, and some with firm design
  To make the lasses martyrs
      With gab that night.

Then first, among the kale so thick,
　Their stalks must all be sought once;
They close their eyes, and grope, and pick,
　For big ones, and for straight ones.
Poor silly Will fell off the drift,
　And wandered through the bow-kale,
And pulled, for want of better shift,
　A stalk was like a sow-tail,
　　So bent that night.

Then, straight or twisted, earth or none
　The noise gets loud and bolder·
The very children, toddling run,
　With stalks out-o'er their shoulder:
To prove if they are sweet or sour,
　They draw their knives and taste them,
Then cosily above the door,
　With careful hands they place them,
　　To lie that night.

The lasses stole off to the ground,
　To pull their stalks of corn;
But Rob slips out, and slinks around
　Behind the big old thorn;
He clutched at Nelly hard and fast,
　The rest screamed like a pack loose;
But her top-pickle, nigh was lost,
　While training in the stackhouse
　　With him that night.

The old goodwife's well-hoarded nuts
　Are round and round divided,
And many lads' and lasses' fates,
　Are there that night decided;
Some kindle sweetly, side by side,
　With no intent of parting;
Some jump away with saucy pride,
　Out-o'er the chimney starting,
　　Full high that night.

Jean slips in two most carefully,
　Who 'twas she would not mention,
But this is Jock, and this is me,
　Was her devout intention;
He blazed o'er her, and she o'er him,
　As if they'd never more part,
Till, fuff! he started with a vim,
　And Jean had e'en a sore heart
　　To see't that night.

Poor Willie, with his bow-kale stalk,
    Was burnt with primsie Mallie;
But Mary's pride received a shock
    To be compared to Willie;
Mall's nut leaped out with prideful fling,
    And her own foot it burnt it;
Then Will jumped up and swore by jing,
    'T was just the way he wanted
            To be that night.

Nell had the stack-house in her mind,
    She puts herself and Rob in;
In loving blaze they 're sweetly joined
    Till white in ash they 're sobbin';
Nell's heart was dancing at the sight
    She whispered Rob to look for 't;
Rob squeezed and kissed her with delight
    Right snugly in the nook for 't,
            Unseen that night.

But Marion sitting at their backs,
    On Andrew Bell was thinking;
Soon leaves them gabbling at their talks
    And out the door went slinking;
Then through the yard she fleetly skims,
    And to the kiln she goes then,
And darkling groped round for the beams
    And in the blue clew throws then,
            Right scared that night.

But still she wound, and still she sweat
    With anxious fear and worry;
Till something held within the pot,
    She thought 't was the Old Harry!
But whether 't was the De'il so fell,
    Or whether 't was a cross-beam,
Or whether it was Andrew Bell —
    She uttered but a low scream
            And fled that night.

Wee Jenny to her granny says:
    "Will you go with me, granny?
I 'll eat the apple at the glass
    I got from Uncle Johnny."
She fuffed her pipe beyond her wont
    In wrath she was so vaporin',
And witnessed not a cinder burnt
    Her bran new worsted apron
            Out through that night.

"You little saucy, brazen face!
  How dare you try such sportin',
As seek the foul thief of the place,
  For him to tell your fortune;
No doubt but you may get a sight!
  Such wicked things are serious,
For many a one has got a fright
  And lived and died delirious
      On such a night.

"One Autumn near the Sherriff-moor—
  I mind it well, I ween;
I was a lassie then, I'm sure
  I was not past fifteen;
The summer had been cold and wet
  And ev'ry thing was green;
And aye a harvest-feast we got,
  And just on Halloween
      It fell that night.

"We had one Rab McGraen, by name,
  A handsome, sturdy fellow,
'Twas he brought Eppie Sim to shame
  That lived at Achmacalla:
To sow hemp-seed got in his head,
  Our warning fears he slighted;
But many a day was out his head,
  He was so sore affrighted
      That very night."

Then up got fighting Jamie Fleck,
  And he swore by his conscience
That he could sow hemp-seed a peck,
  For it was all but nonsense;
Our goodman handed down the sack,
  And out a handful gave him,
Then bade him slip from 'mong the folk,
  When no one did perceive him,
      And try't that night.

He marches through among the stacks,
  Though fear began to blind him;
The pitchfork for a harrow takes,
  And hauls it right behind him;
And ev'ry now and then he says,
  "Hemp-seed I sow thee,
And she that is to be my lass,
  Come after me, and draw thee
      As fast this night."

He whistled up Lord Lenox' march,
  His fears for to dissemble;
Although his hair began to arch,
  And limbs began to tremble:
When presently he hears a squeak,
  And then a grunt and squalling;
Next o'er his shoulder gives a peek,
  And tumbles over bawling
        Full loud that night.

He roared a horrid murder shout,
  In dreadful desperation!
And young and old came running out,
  To hear the sad narration;
He swore 'twas limping Jean McCall,
  Or humpbacked Marion Giggie,
Till, stop! she trotted through them all,
  And who was it but piggy
        Astray that night.

Meg fain would to the barn have gone
  To make believe to winnow,
But for to meet the Deil alone,
  She was as shy's a minnow·
She gave the herd-lad a few nuts,
  And two big, rosy apples,
To watch, while for the barn she sets
  In hopes to see Tom Kipples
        That very night.

She turns the key with anxious care,
  And o'er the threshold ventures;
But first makes sure the lad is near,
  Then boldly in she enters;
A frightened rat run up the wall,
  And she cried Lord, preserve her!
And ran through dung-heap, hole, and all,
  And prayed with zeal and fervor,
        Right fast that night.

The bean-stack charm they then advise
  Will, doubtfully enlisting;
It chanced the stack he fathomed thrice,
  Was timber-propped for twisting;
He took a gnarled old moss-oak,
  For some black devil prying;
Then let an oath and drew a stroke,
  Till skin in shreds went flying
        Off's hands that night.

A wanton widow Lizzie was,
  So kittenish and cunning;
But on that night, alas, poor Liz,
  She got her fill of funning!
She o'er the rocky fells runs fleet,
  Where few would care to live in,
And in the brook, where three farms meet,
  She dips her left shirt-sleeve in,
    That lonesome night.

From rocky shelf the brooklet leaps
  As through the glen it wimples,
Then round the stones and branches creeps,
  Or in an eddy dimples;
It mirrors back fair Luna's rays,
  With flickering, dancing dazzle,
Or glides in darkling, devious ways,
  Beneath the spreading hazel,
    Unseen that night.

Among the ferns upon the bluff,
  Between her and the moon,
The Deil, or else a wandering calf,
  Got up and gave a groan:
Poor Lizzie's heart nigh burst it's shell,
  Up like a lark she bounded,
Then missed her foot, and stumbling fell,
  O'er head and ears dumfounded,
    In th' pool that night.

In order, on the clean hearthstone,
  The dishes three are ranged,
And ev'ry time great care is shown,
  To see them duly changed:
Old Uncle John, who wedlock's joys
  Since Mar's year did desire,
Because his dish was empty thrice,
  He threw them in the fire,
    In wrath that night.

With merry songs, and friendly talks,
  I wot they did not weary;
With fable-tales and funny jokes
  Their sports were cheap and cheery;
Then oatmeal sowens, round they pass,
  So fragrant, hot, and sappy;
And with a hearty, social glass,
  They parted gay and happy,
    For home that night.

AN OLD FARMER'S NEW YEAR'S MORNING
SALUTATION TO HIS OLD MARE MAGGIE.

A good New-Year I wish thee, Meg!
Here, there's a feed for thy old bag;
Though thy old back is bent and scrag,
          I've seen the day
Thou could'st have run like any stag
          Out o'er the way.

Though now thy bones are stiff and crazy,
And thy old hide's as white's a daisy,
I've seen thee dappled, sleek and glossy,
          A bonny gray;
They'd been right smart that dared to face thee,
          Once in a day.

Thou once was in the foremost rank,
A filly, stately, strong and lank,
And set well down a shapely shank,
          As e'er trod earth;
And could'st have leaped right o'er a bank
          Of ample girth.

It's now some nine-and-twenty year,
Since thou was my good father's mare ·
My dower was thee — ten guineas clear,
          And one bright shilling;
Though small, the cash to him was dear
          But he was willing.

When first young Jean my heart was winning,
You with your mammy then was running;
Though you was tricky, sly and cunning,
          Thou ne'er did harm;
'Twas joy to see thee romping, funning,
          Around the farm.

That day, you pranced with conscious pride,
When you bore home my bonny bride ·
And sweet and graceful she did ride,
          With maiden air!
I'd challenge all Kyle-Stewart wide
          For such a pair.

Though now you do but limp and totter,
Like some old nag of some old cotter

That day you was a sprightly trotter,
   For heels and wind!
And left them all in hopeless clutter,
   Far, far behind.

When you and I were young and fair,
And stable meals at fairs were rare,
How thou would prance, and neigh, and flare,
   And take the road!
Till town folks ran with frightened stare,
   And thought thee mad.

When you got corn and I got mellow,
We took the road just like a swallow;
At weddings thou had ne'er a fellow
   For pith and speed;
But ev'ry head thy tail would follow
   O'er hill or mead.

The small, rump-drooping hunter cattle,
Might worse thee in a short bit rattle,
But six Scotch miles! you 've tried their mettle,
   And made them wheeze;
No whip nor spur, but just a whittle
   Cut from the trees.

You was a fine near-horse for ploughing,
As you in front of me kept towing,
Oft thou and me in eight hours going,
   In good March weather,
Have turned six roods, all fine for growing,
   For days together.

Thou never pulled by fits and starts,
But whisked around thy tail in darts;
Then strength, your honest heart imparts
   To willing legs,
Till hardened soil and earthy warts
   Are shapely rigs.

When frosts lay long, and snows were deep,
And threatened labor back to keep,
I gave thy dish a small bit heap
   Of extra filling,
I knew you ne'er would lag nor creep
   But aye be willing.

In cart or car thou never rested,
At steepest hill thou ne'er was worsted,
Thou never leaped, and reared, and twisted,
      Nor stood to blow;
Thy step was just a little hasted,
      Then up you'd go.

My plough-teams are thy children all,
Four gallant brutes as e'er did haul;
Besides **six** more, both strong and tall,
      That thou has foaled;
They brought me thirty pounds in all,
      In yellow gold.

Day after day we two have wrought,
And with the weary world have fought,
And many an anxious time I thought
      We would be beat!
Yet here to crazy age we're brought
      With something yet.

But think not, my old trusty servant,
My love for thee has grown less fervent,
Or in thy stable thou may starve in't,
      For my last spree;
I've promised fair, and will not swerve in't,
      To care for thee.

And now since we've grown old together,
We'll totter round with one another;
With kindly care I'll hitch my tether
      In pleasant meadows,
Where you can hobble free from bother
      Till death o'ershadows.

A DREAM.

[The poet dreams he is at court on George the Third's birthday.]

  " Thoughts, words, and deeds, the statute blames with reason;
    But surely dreams were ne'er indicted treason."

Good-morning to your Majesty!
  May Heaven augment your blisses
On every new birthday you see,
  A humble poet wishes!
My bardship here at your levee,

On such a day as this is,
Is sure an uncouth sight to see
Among those birthday dresses
So fine this day.

I see you're complimented throng,
By many a lord and lady;
"God save the King"'s a cuckoo song
That's easy to be said aye;
The poets, too, a venal gang,
With rhymes well-turned and ready,
Would make you think you ne'er do wrong,
But aye unerring steady,
On such a day.

For me, before a monarch's face
Ev'n there I will not flatter;
For neither pension, post, nor place,
Am I your humble debtor:
So, no reflection on Your Grace,
Your kingship to bespatter,
There's many worse been of the [race,
And maybe some been better
Than you this day.

'T is very true, my sovereign King,
My skill may well be doubted;
But still, a fact's a stubborn thing,
That dare not be disputed.
Your royal nest beneath your wing *
Is e'en right reft and clouted,
And now the third part of the string,
And less will go about it
Than did one day

Far be 't from me that I aspire
To blame your legislation,
Or say you wisdom want, or fire,
To rule this mighty nation!
But, faith! I doubt, my noble Sire,
You've trusted ministration
To chaps, who, on a farm, for hire,
Would better filled their station
Than courts yon day.

And now you've giv'n old Britain peace;
Her broken shins to plaster;
Your sore taxation does her fleece,

* Alluding to the American Revolution.

She scarce a coin can muster;
For me, thank God, my life 's a lease
  No bargain wearing faster,
Or, faith! I fear, that, with the geese,
  I 'll shortly have to pasture
        On fields some day.

I 'm not mistrusting Willie Pitt,
  When taxes he enlarges,
(A worthy sire did him beget
  As ever served the Georges;)
That he intends to pay your debt,
  And lessen all your charges;
But, God-sake! let no saving fit
  Abridge your bonny barges
        And boats this day.

Adieu, my liege! may freedom geck
  Beneath your high protection;
And may you twist corruption's neck,
  And give her for dissection!
But since I 'm here, I won't neglect,
  In loyal, true affection,
To pay your Queen, with due respect,
  My fealty and subjection
        This great birthday.

Hail, Majesty Most Excellent!
  While peers pretend to love you,
Will you accept a compliment
  A simple bard would give you?
Your children dear, that Heaven has lent,
  Still higher may they move you
In blissful hope, till Death consent,
  Forever to relieve you
        From care that day.

For you, young potentate of Wales, *
  I tell Your Highness fairly,
Down pleasure's stream, with swelling sails,
  I 'm told you 're driving rarely;
But some day you may gnaw your nails,
  And curse your follies early,
The time you broke Diana's pales,
  And rattled dice with Charlie †
        By night or day.

---

* Afterwards George IV.
† Charles James Fox.

Yet oft a wayward colt's been known
  At last to win our favor;
So you may fitly fill a throne,
  When wiser grown and graver.
There's him at Agincourt who shone,*
  Few better were or braver,
Yet with that lusty knave, Sir John,†
  He was a queer young shaver
      For many a day.

For you, right reverend Osnaburg,‡
  None sets the lawn-sleeve sweeter,
Although a ribbon on your leg
  Would been a dress completer;
As you disown yon pious rogue
  That bears the keys of Peter,
Then, quick, and get a wife to hug!
  Or troth! you'll stain the mitre
      Some luckless day

Young, Tarry Hands, your Grace I learn §
  Has lately come athwart her;
A glorious galley, stem and stern
  Well rigged for Venus' barter;
But first hang out, that she'll discern
  Your hymeneal charter,
Then heave aboard your grappling iron,
  And, large upon her quarter,
      Come full that day.

And, lastly, bonny blossoms all,
  Ye royal lasses dainty,
May you be wise and good withal
  And have of suitors plenty;
First give our British boys a call,
  For kings are rather scant aye;
Yet, German Princes, though but small,
  Are better still than want aye
      On any day.

---

* Shakespeare's *Prince Hal.*
† Sir John Falstaff.
‡ Frederick, second son of George III., who in his early years was Bishop of Osnaburg.
§ William, Duke of Clarence, afterwards William IV., and allusion to a youthful intrigue. He was in the navy in early life.

God bless you all! consider now,
  You 're flattered and exalted;
But ere the course of life be through,
  It may be bitter salted·
I, in my time, have seen a few
  Whose cup with pleasure malted;
Have drank the dregs with mournful rue,
  When Fortune's favors halted
    Some later day.

THE VISION — DUAN FIRST.

The sun had closed the winter day,
The curlers quit their roaring play,
And hungry hares gone up the way
    To kale-yards green,
While faithless snows each step betray
    Where they have been.

The weary flail I had been swinging,
The long day's toil, small comfort bringing·
So when the sun his course was winging
    Far in the west,
I homeward went, at curfew ringing,
    To sit and rest.

There lonely by the fire-side cheek,
I watched the winds descending freak,
That filled with cough-provoking reek,
    The old clay cottage,
And heard the walled rat's hungry squeak,
    At smell of pottage.

All in this smoky, murky clime,
I backward mused on wasted time,
How I had spent my youthful prime,
    Devoid of sense;
There 's neither fame in idle rhyme,
    Nor recompense.

Had I of sense had but a part,
I might have prospered in the mart,
Or trusted to the bank, right smart,
    My cash account;
Now, crazed, half-fed, with scarce a shirt,
    Is all th' amount.

Then, fool! I loud myself did brand,
And heaved on high my horny hand,
To swear by all yon stars so grand,
    Or some rash oath,
That rhymes, henceforth, I would withstand
    Till latest breath.

When click! the latch announced a call.
And back the door went to the wall,
Then quick I saw step in the hall,
    By bright fire-light,
A tight outlandish hussy, tall,
    Come full in sight.

You need not doubt my voice was hushed
The infant oath, half-formed was crushed,
My eyes nigh out their sockets gushed
    With frightened mien:
When sweet, like modest Worth, she blushed
    And stepped right in.

Green, slender, leaf-clad holly-boughs
Were twisted graceful round her brows;
I took her for some Scottish Muse,
    By that same token:
And come to stop those reckless vows,
    Would soon be broken.

A hair-brained sentimental trace,
Was strongly pictured in her face,
A wildly-witty rustic grace
    Shone full upon her:
Her soulful look on empty space,
    Beamed high with honor.

Down flowed her robe of tartan sheen
Till scarcely half a leg was seen;
And such a leg! my bonny Jean
    Could only peer it:
So straight, so taper, tight and clean
    None else came near it.

Her mantle large, of greenish hue,
My gazing wonder chiefly drew;
Deep lights and shades, bold-mingling threw
    A lustre grand;
And seem'd, to my astonish'd view,
    A well-known land.

Here, rivers in the sea were lost;
There, mountains to the skies were tost;
Here, tumbling billows mark'd the coast
          With surging foam;
There, distant shone Art's lofty boast,
          The lordly dome.

Here, Doon pour'd down his far-fetch'd floods;
There, well-fed Irwine stately thuds;
Old hermit Ayr stole through his woods,
          On to the shore;
And many a lesser torrent scuds,
          With seeming roar.

Low, in a sandy valley spread,
An ancient borough rear'd her head;
Still, as in Scottish story read,
          She boasts a race
To ev'ry nobler virtue bred,
          And polish'd grace.

By stately tow'r or palace fair,
Or ruins pendent in the air,
Bold stems of heroes, here and there
          I could discern;
Some seemed to muse, some seemed to dare,
          With features stern.

My heart did glowing transport feel,
To see a race heroic wheel,
And brandish round the deep-dy'd steel
          In sturdy blows;
While back-recoiling seem'd to reel
          Their Suthron foes.

His Country's Savior, mark him well!
Bold Richardton's heroic swell;
The chief on Sark who glorious fell,
          In high command;
And he whom ruthless fates expel
          His native land.

There, where a sceptred Pictish shade
Stalk'd round his ashes lowly laid,
I mark'd a martial race, portray'd
          In colors strong;
Bold, soldier-featured, undismayed
          They strode along.

Through many ,a wild, romantic grove,
Near many a hermit-fancied cove,
(Fit haunts for friendship or for love,)
    In musing mood,
An aged judge, I saw him rove,
    Dispensing good.

With deep-struck, reverential awe
The learned sire and son I saw,
To Nature's God and Nature's law
    They gave their lore,
This, all its source and end to draw;
    That, to adore.

Brydone's brave ward I well could spy,
Beneath old Scotia's smiling eye;
Who call'd on Fame, low standing by,
    To hand him on,
Where many a patriot name on high
    And hero shone.

DUAN SECOND.

With musing-deep, astonish'd stare,
I view'd the heavenly seeming fair;
A whispering throb did witness bear
    Of kindred sweet,
When with an elder sister's air
    She did me greet: —

" All hail! my own inspired bard!
In me thy native Muse regard;
Nor longer mourn thy fate is hard,
    Thus poorly low!
I come to give thee such reward
    As we bestow.

" Know, the great genius of this land
Has many a light, aerial band,
Who, all beneath his high command,
    Harmoniously,
As arts or arms they understand,
    Their labors ply.

"They Scotia's race among them share;
Some fire the soldier on to dare:
Some rouse the patriot up to bare
      Corruption's heart:
Some teach the bard a darling care,
      The tunefu' art.

"'Mong swelling floods of reeking gore,
They ardent, kindling spirits pour;
Or, 'mid the venal senate's roar,
      They, sightless, stand,
To mend the honest patriot-lore,
      And grace the hand.

"And when the bard, or hoary sage,
Charm or instruct the future age,
They bind the wild, poetic rage,
      In energy,
Or point the inconclusive page
      Full on the eye.

"Hence Fullarton, the brave and young;
Hence Dempster's zeal-inspired tongue;
Hence sweet harmonious Beattie sung
      His 'Minstrel Lays;'
Or tore, with noble ardor stung,
      The sceptic's bays.

"To lower orders are assign'd
The humbler ranks of humankind
The rustic bard, the lab'ring hind,
      The artisan;
All choose as various they're inclin'd,
      The various man.

"When yellow waves the heavy grain,
The threat'ning storm some strongly rein;
Some teach to meliorate the plain
      With tillage skill;
And some instruct the shepherd train,
      Blithe o'er the hill.

"Some hint the lover's harmless wile;
Some grace the maiden's artless smile;
Some soothe the lab'rer's weary toil
      For humble gains,
And make his cottage scenes beguile
      His cares and pains.

"Some, bounded to a district space,
Explore at large man's infant race,
To mark the embryotic trace
    Of rustic bard;
And careful note each op'ning grace
    A guide and guard.

"Of these am I — COILA my name;
And this district as mine I claim,
Where once the Campbells, chiefs of fame,
    Held ruling pow'r;
I mark'd thy embryo tuneful flame,
    Thy natal hour.

"With future hope, I oft would gaze
Fond, on thy little early ways,
Thy, rudely-caroll'd, chiming phrase,
    In uncouth rhymes,
Fir'd at the simple, artless lays
    Of other times.

"I saw thee seek the sounding shore,
Delighted with the dashing roar;
Or when the North his fleecy store
    Drove thro' the sky,
I saw grim Nature's visage hoar.
    Struck thy young eye.

"Or when the deep green-mantl'd earth
Warm-cherish'd ev'ry flow'ret's birth,
And joy and music pouring forth
    In ev'ry grove,
I saw thee eye the gen'ral mirth
    With boundless love.

"When ripen'd fields, and azure skies,
Call'd forth the reapers' rustling noise,
I saw thee leave their ev'ning joys,
    And lonely stalk,
To vent thy bosom's swelling, rise.
    In pensive walk,

When youthful love, warm-blushing, strong,
Keen-shivering shot thy nerves along,
Those accents, grateful to thy tongue,
    Th' adored Name,
I taught thee how to pour in song,
    To soothe thy flame.

" I saw thy pulse's maddening play,
Wild send thee Pleasure's devious way,
Misled by Fancy's meteor ray,
          By passion driven;
But yet the light that led astray
          Was light from Heaven.

" I taught thy manners-painting strains,
The loves, the ways of simple swains,
Till now, o'er all my wide domains
          Thy fame extends;
And some, the pride of Coila's plains,
          Become thy friends.

" Thou canst not learn, nor can I show
To paint with Thomson's landscape glow;
Or wake the bosom-melting throe
          With Shenstone's art.
Or pour, with Gray, the moving flow
          Warm on the heart.

" Yet all beneath the unrivall'd rose,
The lowly daisy sweetly blows;
Tho' large the forest's monarch throws
          His army shade,
Yet green the juicy hawthorn grows
          Adown the glade.

" Then never murmur nor repine;
Strive in thy humble sphere to shine;
And trust me, not Potosi's mine,
          Nor king's regard,
Can give a bliss o'ermatching thine,
          A rustic bard!

" To give my counsels all in one,—
Thy tuneful flame still careful fan·
Preserve the dignity of man
          With soul erect;
And trust the Universal Plan
          Will all protect.

" And wear thou this," she solemn said,
And bound the holly round my head;
The polish'd leaves, and berries red,
          Did rustling play;
And, like a passing thought, she fled
          In light away.

THE TREE OF LIBERTY.

Heard you of the tree of France?
  I wot not what the name is;
Around it all the patriots dance,
  In Europe it is famous.
It stands where once the Bastile stood,
  A prison built by kings, man,
When Superstition's hellish brood
  Kept France in leading strings, man.

Upon this tree there grows a fruit
  You cannot buy with pelf, man;
It raises man above the brute,
  It makes him know himself, man.
If once the peasant taste a bit
  He's greater than a lord, man,
And with the beggar shares a mite
  Of all he can afford, man.

This fruit is worth all Afric's wealth;
  To comfort us 't was sent, man,
To give the sweetest blush of health,
  And make us all content, man.
It clears the eyes, it cheers the heart;
  Makes high and low good friends, man;
And he who acts the traitor's part
  It to perdition sends, man.

May blessings always on him wait
  Who pitied Gallia's slaves, man,
And stole a branch, in spite of fate,
  From o'er the western waves, man.
Fair Virtue watered it with care,
  And now she sees with pride, man,
How well it buds and blossoms there,
  Its branches spreading wide, man.

But kings and courts still hate to see
  The works of Freedom thrive, man,
And of the fruit of this fair tree
  They fain would us deprive, man.
King Louis thought to cut it down
  When it was young and small, man;
For this the watchman cracked his crown,
  Cut off his head and all, man.

A wicked crew then, bent on crime,
  Did take a solemn oath, man,
It ne'er should flourish in its prime,
  To which they pledged their troth, man;
Away they went with mock parade,
  Like beagles hunting game, man,
But soon grew weary of the trade,
  And came to grief and shame, man.

For Freedom, standing by the tree,
  Her sons did loudly call, man;
She sang a song of liberty,
  Which pleased them one and all, man.
By her inspired, the new-born race
  Soon drew the avenging steel, man;
The hirelings ran — her foes gave chase,
  And made the despots reel, man.

Let Britain boast her hardy oak,
  Her poplar and her pine, man,
Old Britain once could crack her joke,
  And o'er her neighbors shine, man;
But seek the forest round and round,
  And soon 'twill be agreed, man,
That such a tree cannot be found,
  'Tween London and the Tweed, man.

Without this tree, alack! this life
  Is but a vale of woe, man,
A scene of sorrow mixed with strife,
  No real joys we know, man.
We labor soon, we labor late,
  To feed the titled knave, man,
And all the comfort we're to get
  Is that beyond the grave, man.

With plenty of such trees, I trow,
  The world would live in peace, man;
The sword would help to make a plough,
  The din of war would cease, man.
Like brethren in a common cause,
  We'd on each other smile, man,
And equal rights and equal laws
  Would gladden every isle, man.

Ill fare the loon who would not eat
　Such wholesome, dainty cheer, man;
I 'd give my shoes from off my feet
　To taste such fruit, I swear, man.
Then let us pray old England may
　Sure plant this famous tree, man,
And loud we 'll sing and hail the day
　That gave us liberty, man.

ADDRESS OF BEELZEBUB TO THE PRESIDENT OF THE HIGHLAND SOCIETY.

* [It appears that at a meeting of the Highland Society, in London, Earl
of Breadalbane President, measures were taken to frustrate the designs of
five hundred Highlanders, who, as the society were informed by Mr.
M———of A———s, were so audacious as to attempt to escape from their
lawful lords and masters, whose property they were, by emigrating from
the lands of Mr. McDonald of Glengarry, to the wilds of Canada, in search
of that fantastic thing — "LIBERTY." It must be kept in mind that the
lines are Beelzebub's, to the President.]

Long life, my lord, and health be yours
Unscathed by hunger'd Highland boors;
Lord, grant no tattered desperate beggar,
With dirk, claymore, or rusty trigger,
Should sever Scotland from a life
She likes — as lambkins like the knife.
Faith! you and A———s were right
To keep the Highland hounds in sight:
I doubt not! they would like no better
Than let them once out o'er the water;
Then up among those lakes and seas
They 'll make what rules and laws they please;
Some daring Hancock, or a Franklin,
May set their Highland blood a-ranklin'·
Some Washington again may head them,
Or some Montgomery, fearless lead them,
Till God knows what may be effected
When by such heads and hearts directed.
Poor dunghill sons of dirt and mire
May to Patrician rights aspire!
No sage North now, nor sager Sackville,
To watch and premier o'er the pack vile.
And where will you get Howes and Clintons
To bring them to a right repentance,
To cowe the rebel generation,
And save the honor of the nation?

They, and be d———d! what right have they
To meat or sleep, or light of day?
Far less to riches, power, or freedom,
Or what your lordship may forbid 'em ?
But hear, my lord! Glengarry, hear!
Your hand 's o'er light on them, I fear!
Your bailiffs, trustees, and such fellows,
I cannot say but they are zealous
In carrying out their legal function —
They rasp the loons without compunction;
Yet, while they 're only taxed and pounded,
Their Highland grit is deeper grounded ·
But smash and crash the stubborn lot;
In debtors' jails, there let them rot!
The young dogs, thrash them to their labor
Till work and hunger make them sober!
The hussies, if they 're young and pretty,
Dispatch them off to London City!
And if the wives and dirty brats
Are clamoring at your doors and gates,
Their fluttering duds with vermin swarming,
Your lordship's ducks and geese alarming;
Just ply your whip, and do not spare them ·
Call out your dogs to bite and scare them,
And make the tattered gypsies pack
With all their bastards on their back!
Go on, my lord! I long to meet you,
And in my house at home to greet you:
With common lords you won't be mingled,
A hotter place for you I 've singled,
At my right hand assigned your seat,
'Tween Herod's hip and Polycrate —
Or, if this does not melt your marrow,
Between Almagro and Pizzaro,
A seat, I 'm sure you 're well deservin 't:
And till you come — Your humble servant

                                    BEELZEBUB.

June 1, Anno Mundi 5700 [A. D. 1786].

AULD LANG SYNE.

Should auld acquaintance be forgot,
   Dear friend and comrade, mine?
Should auld acquaintance be forgot,
   And the days of auld lang syne?

CHORUS.

For auld lang syne, my dear,
   For auld lang syne,
We 'll take a cup of kindness yet,
   For the days of auld lang syne.

We two have run about the hills,
   And pulled the blossoms fine;
But we 've wandered many a weary foot
   Since the days of auld lang syne.—CHORUS.

We two have played within the brook
   From morning sun till dine;
But seas between us broad have roared
   Since the days of auld lang syne. — CHORUS.

And there 's a hand my trusty friend,
   Give me that hand of thine;
And we 'll take a hearty bumper yet,
   For the days of auld lang syne. — CHORUS.

And surely I 'll partake with you,
   And you'll partake of mine;
And we'll take a cup of kindness yet
   For the days of auld lang syne. — CHORUS.

THERE WAS A LAD WAS BORN IN KYLE.

There was a lad was born in Kyle,
But on what day or what the style,
I think it 's hardly worth my while
   To be so nice with Robin.
     Robin was a rovin' boy,
      Rantin' rovin', rantin' rovin';
     Robin was a rovin' boy,
      Rantin' rovin' Robin.

Our Monarch's hindmost year but one
Was five and twenty days begun,
'T was then a streak of wintry sun
   Glanced kindly in on Robin.— CHORUS.

The gipsy gossip viewed his hand;
Quoth she " Who lives must understand
His fame will echo round the land;
  I think we 'll call him Robin.—CHORUS.

" He 'll have misfortunes great and small,
But yet a heart above them all;
He 'll be a credit to us all,
  We 'll all be proud of Robin.—CHORUS.

" And sure as three times three make nine,
I see by ev'ry score and line,
To all our kindred he 'll incline,
  Which makes me fond of Robin.—CHORUS.

" And faith ! I see that he 's destined
To work mischief with womankind,
For which he will be sore maligned,
  But blessings on thee, Robin."—CHORUS.

JOHN ANDERSON, MY JO.

John Anderson, my jo, John,
  When we were newly wed,
Your hair was like the raven,
  Your cheeks were round and red;
But now your cheeks are thin, John,
  Your locks are like the snow;
Yet blessings on your old gray head,
  John Anderson, my jo.

John Anderson, my jo, John,
  We 've climbed the hill together,
And many a happy day, John,
  We 've had with one another;
Now we must totter down, John,
  But hand in hand we 'll go,
And sleep together at the foot,
  John Anderson, my jo.

TAM GLEN.

Dear sister, my heart it is breaking
  For one of the best of good men;
Ah, surely my peace he is wrecking,
  And what will I do with Tam Glen.

I think I might wed the dear fellow,
  Though poor is his lot, even then·
What care I in riches to wallow
  If I must not marry Tam Glen.

There's Lawrie, the laird of Dalwhinny,
  As cross as a bear in his den:
He brags and he blows of his money,
  But when will he dance like Tam Glen.
My mother does constantly deave me,
  And bids me beware of young men;
They flatter, she says, to deceive me,
  But who can think so of Tam Glen.

My father says, if I 'll forsake him,
  He 'll give me of good guineas ten;
But, if it 's ordained I must take him,
  Oh, who will I get like Tam Glen?
Last night at the valentines' dealing,
  My heart leaped again and again,
For thrice I drew one, without failing,
  And thrice it was written, Tam Glen.

On last Halloween I lay waking,
  I dipped my left sleeve, you know when;
His likeness came up the house stalking,
  And the very gray suit of Tam Glen.
Come counsel, dear sister! don't tarry
  I 'll give you my bonny black hen,
If you will advise me to marry
  The lad I love dearly — Tam Glen

———

O WHY SHOULD HONEST POVERTY.

O why should honest poverty,
  Hang down his head, and all that?
The coward slave, we pass him by,
  And dare be poor, for all that!
For all that, and all that;
  Our toils obscure, and all that;
The rank is but the guinea-stamp,
  The man 's the gold for all that.

What though on humble fare we dine,
  Wear homely gray and all that;
Give fools their silks and knaves their wine,
  A man's a man for all that!
For all that, and all that,
  Their tinsel show, and all that;
The honest man, though e'er so poor,
  Is king of men for all that!

You see yon upstart, called a lord,
  Who struts, and stares, and all that;
Though hundreds worship at his word,
  He's but a dunce for all that:
For all that, and all that,
  His riband, star, and all that;
The man of independent mind,
  He looks and laughs at all that!

A king can make a belted knight,
  A marquis, duke, and all that;
Bnt an honest man's above his might,
  Good faith, he must not fall that!
For all that, and all that,
  Their dignities, and all that,
The pith of sense, and pride of worth,
  Are higher ranks than all that.

Then let us pray that come it may —
  As come it will for all that —
That sense and worth, o'er all the earth,
  Will honored be, and all that.
For all that, and all that,
  It's coming yet for all that,
When man to man the wide world o'er,
  Shall brothers be and all that.

TO MARY IN HEAVEN.

[For the benefit of those who are not familiar with the life of Burns, I append two songs; one of which is in English, and the other nearly so.

"To Mary in Heaven," was composed on the anniversary of the death of the unfortunate Mary Campbell, a rustic Highland lassie of rare beauty, personally, and of great sweetness and amiability of character. The name of " Highland Mary " is revered in Scotland, by old and young, with a sainted regard. Burns was betrothed to her (in the manner described in the song, somewhat,) and she was on her way to meet him, when their marriage was to have taken place ; on arriving at Greenock, she was seized with a malignant fever, and died after two or three days' illness and before word could reach her lover.

The songs of " Highland Mary " and " Flow gently, sweet Afton," are examples of the undying impression she made and left on the Poet's inmost being. All his other loves, and they were many, pale before his love for this sweet soul. Her name, as linked with his, is hallowed in every household in their native land.]

Thou ling'ring star, with less'ning ray,
    That lov'st to greet the early morn,
Again thou usher'st in the day
    My Mary from my soul was torn.
O Mary! dear departed shade!
    Where is thy place of blissful rest?
See'st thou thy lover lowly laid?
    Hear'st thou the groans that rend his breast?

That sacred hour can I forget?
    Can I forget the hallow'd grove,
Where, by the winding Ayr, we met,
    To live one day of parting love?
Eternity will not efface
    Those records dear of transports past;
Thy image at our last embrace —
    Ah! little thought we 't was our last!

Ayr, gurgling, kissed his pebbled shore,
    O'erhung with wild woods, thick'ning, green,
The fragrant birch and hawthorn hoar
    Twined am'rous round the raptured scene.
The flowers sprang wanton to be prest;
    The birds sang love on ev'ry spray;
Till too, too soon, the glowing west
    Proclaim'd the speed of wingèd day.

Still o'er these scenes my mem'ry wakes,
    And fondly broods with miser care!
Time but the impression stronger makes,
    As streams their channels deeper wear.
My Mary! dear departed shade!
    Where is thy place of blissful rest?
See'st thou thy lover lowly laid?
    Hear'st thou the groans that rend his breast?

AE FOND KISS.

[" Ae Fond Kiss," is addressed to Clarinda, — otherwise, Mrs. Agnes McLehose, a lady of great beauty of person, character, and accomplishment, that the poet formed a strong predilection for.   Her husband had deserted her for foreign parts, but was still living; which, naturally, made the meeting and correspondence of Burns and the lady " sub rosa." The letters that passed between them show a good deal of fine fencing on delicate ground; and, that a warmer sentiment than friendship was imminent, is shown by the final parting evidenced in the song.]

Ae fond kiss, and then we sever;
Ae fareweel, and then, forever!
Deep in heart-wrung tears I'll pledge thee,
Warring sighs and groans I'll wage thee.

Who shall say that Fortune grieves him,
While the star of hope she leaves him?
Me, nae cheerfu' twinkle lights me;
Dark despair around benights me.

I'll ne'er blame my partial fancy,
Naething could resist my Nancy;
But to see her was to love her;
Love but her, and love forever.

Had we never loved sae kindly,
Had we never loved sae blindly,
Never met — or never parted,
We had ne'er been broken-hearted.

Fare-thee-weel, thou first and fairest!
Fare-thee-weel, thou best and dearest!
Thine be ilka joy and treasure,
Peace, Enjoyment, Love, and Pleasure!

Ae fond kiss, and then we sever·
Ae fareweel, alas! forever!
Deep in heart-wrung tears I'll pledge thee,
Warring sighs and groans I'll wage thee.

CPSIA information can be obtained at www.ICGtesting.com
Printed in the USA
BVOW05s1052010216

435000BV00023B/286/P

9 781331 469544